Empiricism and History

Stephen Davies

palgrave

First published 2003 by
PALGRAVE MACMILLAN
Houndmills, Basingstoke, Hampshire RG21 6XS and
175 Fifth Avenue, New York, N.Y. 10010
Companies and representatives throughout the world

PALGRAVE MACMILLAN is the global academic imprint of the Palgrave
Macmillan division of St. Martin's Press LLC and of Palgrave Macmillan Ltd.
Macmillan® is a registered trademark in the United States, United Kingdom
and other countries. Palgrave is a registered trademark in the European
Union and other countries.

ISBN 0–333–96470–5 paperback

This book is printed on paper suitable for recycling and made from fully
managed and sustained forest sources.

A catalogue record for this book is available from the British Library.

Library of Congress Cataloging-in-Publication Data

Davies, Stephen, 1955–
  Empiricism and history / Stephen Davies.
    p. cm. – (Theory and history)
  Includes bibliographical references and index.
  ISBN 0–333–96470–5 (pbk.)
    1. History–Philosophy. 2. Empiricism. 3. Historiography. 4. Experience–
History. 5. History–Study and teaching. I. Title. II. Series.

D16.8.D27 2003
901–dc21   2002044817

10   9   8   7   6   5   4   3   2   1
12   11   10   09   08   07   06   05   04   03

Typeset in Great Britain by
Aarontype Ltd, Easton, Bristol

Printed in China

Contents

Introduction

▶ Empiricism and debates about history

All of us have beliefs and ideas which shape the way we act and behave. Historians are no exception to this rule. As well as some beliefs they share with their fellow citizens, they have others, largely peculiar to themselves, about the nature of their discipline and their professional activity. It is these ideas, about such matters as the nature of historical knowledge, the form of historical investigation, and the purpose of historical research, which underlie their day to day work. Historians have always been aware of this in general terms. However, it is fair to say that history is an undertheorized discipline, its practitioners not generally concerned to explore the methodological foundations of their subject. Recently, this has changed.

For the last 200 years at least, most historians have drawn their professional ideas and beliefs from one theory. This is **empiricism**. The central doctrine of empiricism, that true knowledge of the world comes ultimately from sense impressions, underlies most of the practices and arguments of professional historians. Empiricism is a doctrine of **epistemology**. That is, it is an answer to the question: 'What do we know (or can we know) and how do we know it?' Any person who makes a factual statement about the world has to be able to answer the question 'How do you know that?' Empiricism is the argument that our knowledge of the world depends upon, and is derived from, experience or observation; that is, the evidence of the senses. The experience that gives knowledge can be direct and unmediated or indirect, via the testimony of another person or persons. So the answer to the question given above could be either, 'Because I personally experienced/observed something' or 'Because someone else's experience/observation was relayed to me'. Empiricism implies the **correspondence theory of truth**. This states that a proposition or idea is true if, and in so far as, it corresponds to a physical reality and that it is perceptions, direct or relayed, which tell us if an idea or proposition corresponds to reality. This means that empiricism is not just a **theory** of knowledge. It is also a theory of how we acquire knowledge. It means that true knowledge of the world can come only from physical experimentation and investigation, rather than other sources such as introspection.

Typically, when ideas are unquestioned and taken for granted they remain inarticulate, existing only in the realm of 'common sense'. It is only when beliefs are challenged that their defenders are driven to spell them out clearly, to search for their foundational assumptions and to elaborate their implications and applications. The case of history shows this very clearly. Despite the challenges of **Marxism** and **social theory** of all kinds, most historians have remained wedded to the one theory, that of empiricism. However, this doctrine has remained undertheorized until recently because of its relative immunity from attack from within the profession. Consequently, many historians have denied that there is a theory behind what they do: instead, professional practices are defended on the grounds that they are common sense, that is, self-evidently correct.

For many years such debate as did take place over historical methodology was between a robust empiricism, articulated by authors such as Sir Geoffrey Elton and Arthur Marwick, and a more theory oriented argument put by writers such as E. H. Carr. As recently as 1991, John Tosh advised his readers that the works of Carr and Elton were the best introduction to this topic, along with Bloch's *The Historians' Craft*. As the most recent edition of Tosh's work makes clear, things have changed.[1]

The cause of this is the impact of the 'linguistic turn' and **postmodernism** upon the discipline of history and its self-perception. For many historians this has been highly unwelcome – Sir Geoffrey Elton went so far as to describe postmodernists as the intellectual equivalent of drug dealers![2] While comfortable about, and capable of dealing with, traditional queries about inevitable partiality or distorted perspective, they are discomforted by the more fundamental questioning and radical scepticism of the postmodernists, with their challenge to the very idea of **'history'** as the profession understands it. The initial response, articulated by authors such as Elton and Marwick, was to reassert the importance of correct method and practice. This, however, missed the point of the argument and is increasingly seen as inadequate.

The result has been a series of more profound defences of the established concept of history and the practice of historical writing and research. In these the older debate between Carr and Elton is put to one side. This reflects the realisation that, when compared to the postmodernists, they agree as much as they differ. In tone these more recent works are often highly polemical, to the point of being intemperate. (Revealingly, this unites traditional left and right in attacking postmodernists.) The most important are Richard Evans's *In Defence of History* and Keith Windschuttle's *The Killing of History*. Marwick has also returned to the fray with a completely rewritten book called, appropriately, *The New Nature of History*.[3] These authors address the arguments of the postmodernist critics directly. They try to spell out what the traditional practice and way of thinking shared by almost all historians is, and to defend it as both possible and virtuous. What was once unarticulated assumption is now being spelt out and made explicit.

Even so, the main focus of Evans and Windschuttle is to attack and rebut the postmodernists rather than to explicate the philosophical basis of history. Marwick, however, does shift the balance with an extensive discussion of the philosophical foundations of historical practice. It is clear from all of these that empiricism remains the predominant, central theory of most **historiography** and research method. Apparently, the ultimate effect of postmodernism has been to make historians more self-conscious about the methodological underpinnings of their professional practice rather than to bring about any general reassessment. This should not surprise us. As we shall see, the very discipline of history as we now understand it came about as a result of applying empirical methods to the study of the past.

What is (surprisingly) not given much attention is the historicity of empirical historiography itself, an historical analysis of the way that this type of thinking about the past and our knowledge of it came to be. Such an analysis reveals several things, including a repeated tendency for historians to explore other ways of approaching historical topics before reverting to the empirical mode, and a movement to apply this method to an ever-wider range of areas. This book, then, tries to do three things. First, to set out very simply what the main elements of the empirical theory of historical knowledge are, along with their implications. Second, to describe how this way of thinking about the past came into existence, initially as an alternative to other ways of understanding the past such as **myth** and tradition. Third, to look at how it has been applied in a number of key areas and how the scope and application of the empirical method have grown over time. This means looking at particular works and historiographical debates not necessarily because of their relevance today, but because they exemplify the way that empirical methods were applied and their persistence in the face of challenge. Consequently, not all of the debates or traditions explored later will be 'alive' or continuing.

▶ Empiricism, knowledge and induction

Empiricism is the belief that true knowledge comes only from sensory experience. This has broad destructive implications for ideas about knowledge which have historically been widely held. It means that knowledge is not the same as belief or opinion. It is not the same thing as certainty, no matter how passionately felt. The emphasis upon experience as the source of knowledge means that other possible **sources** are slighted or rejected. For most empiricist philosophers, pure reason or introspection can only prove the truth of **propositions** that are true by definition and therefore do not require reference to the physical world for confirmation. (An example of this would be a statement such as 'all black objects are not white'.) Since knowledge comes from experience there can be no innate ideas or knowledge, that is, knowledge that precedes, or is independent of, experience. Hence, **intuition** is not a valid source of knowledge. For the empiricist, religious revelation can only be true or be the source of knowledge (as opposed to faith) in so far as its statements can be confirmed by experience. More generally, the same is true for any kind of statement which rests its claim to truth on an appeal to authority or tradition. In fact, although empiricism is nowadays under attack for claiming that we can know more than is actually possible, its principal effect is to create scepticism about most of the claims to knowledge that have been made in the past, and even today.

However, it is important to point out what empiricism does not mean. It does not mean that **theory** or **hypothesis** has no place in knowledge or the discovery of knowledge. What empiricism does mean is that empirical **facts** (knowledge derived from experience) trump hypothesis or theory. If your theory predicts that the sun rises in the West but experience tells you that it actually rises in the East, it is the theory that gives way and is either amended or rejected. Theory is important, however, in making sense of the variety of experience and in suggesting patterns of investigation which lead to greater knowledge. Empiricism also means that facts precede theory and general rules rather than the other way round. We do not construct a theory on the basis of pure reason and then look for facts to confirm it. Rather, we should construct theories or general rules on the basis of empirical knowledge.

This leads to another aspect of empiricism: its connection with the **inductive** mode of reasoning. **Induction** is a term taken from logic and is contrasted with **deduction**. In deductive reasoning one starts with a general statement or **premiss**, followed by a second or minor premiss, usually more specific. An argument is then made, following strict rules, which leads to a conclusion. (An example: Oranges are edible, this fruit is an orange, and therefore this fruit is edible.)[4] As long as the premisses are true and the form of the argument is correct, then the conclusion *must* be true. The movement in a deductive argument is from the general to the specific. Induction by contrast proceeds from the specific case to the general case. In the example given above an observer, after finding that many fruits with similar characteristics were edible, would conclude that such fruits were edible as a general rule. (The inductive argument would be: 'All of the orange fruits I have experienced were edible. This fruit is orange. Therefore this fruit is edible.') The point of course is that conclusions drawn from induction are much less certain than well-founded deductive ones. A hundred specific instances of a phenomenon might have led you to a conclusion only for the hundred and first to not fit it. The classic example of this is the one given by Sir Karl Popper. Observation would lead one to conclude that all swans were white. However, it would only take one black swan, spotted on a trip to Australia, to overthrow that conclusion.

This means that the conclusions drawn from inductive reasoning are held to be true in a tentative way. Many philosophers have argued that the inevitable outcome of the empirical theory of knowledge is radical **scepticism** and despair over the possibility of knowing anything with certainty. The problem with this argument is that it does not allow for degrees of certainty or uncertainty. A stark contrast is made between absolute, certain knowledge on one side, and total lack of certainty about what can be known on the other. However, the degree of tentativeness can vary from the very uncertain, to as certain as can be imagined. Inductive reasoning seeks to move from less to greater certainty. (It is this movement in the direction of certainty that removes the supposed problem of infinite regress in the pursuit of knowledge.)[5]

This is done through the **inductive cycle**. The pattern is as follows: investigation of particular cases leads to an accumulation of knowledge about those particular cases which generates a general conclusion or hypothesis; this generates a question or research programme; the findings that result from this lead to the original explanation being modified; this in turn generates a further set of questions, which lead to further amendment. This often has two consequences. The original hypothesis typically becomes increasingly qualified and complex and may even break down completely, and the investigative questions typically become more precise and concerned with more specific matters in each phase of the cycle. However, the most important outcome is for the area of relative certainty to increase. As we will see, this pattern is found in all of the areas where empirical methods have been applied in the study of the past, that is in history.

Why, though, is there a connection between empiricism as a theory of knowledge and induction as a method of acquiring and organizing knowledge? The reason is straightforward. If knowledge comes from experience, then human beings can have true knowledge only of particulars. We do not directly experience categories such as 'oranges', only specific individual oranges. Induction is the reasoning process that organizes and makes sense of these experiences and creates categories that organize the knowledge gained from sense data into concepts.[6] The upshot of all this is that discrete 'facts' (truth statements that can be confirmed by experience) come first. Theory comes second and may generate further 'facts', but is subordinate to them. It is precisely this that the critics of empiricism attack.

► Empirical knowledge and the human past

If we can say these things about empiricism in general, what are its implications for the study of the past and our knowledge of the past, that is, for the discipline of history? The starting point is the fact derived from experience, that events occur in time, and that time can be divided into past, present and future. Events can be located in time, in relation to one another and to the present. History is the study of the past, specifically the human past. There are peculiar difficulties in the study of the past from an empiricist perspective. The main one is that the past cannot be experienced directly beyond the lifetime of a living observer. Therefore, our knowledge of the past is indirect and rests upon the testimony of evidence that has survived to the present. (It is worth pointing out that history is not unique in this respect. The same point can be made about several of the natural sciences, notably geology, palaeontology and astronomy.) A pessimistic view would be that the past is radically unknowable and is separated from us by the impenetrable veil of time. However, the application of empiricism to the study of the past leads to the conclusion that we can, sometimes, acquire knowledge of the past and therefore make statements about it which are (in the sense described above) 'true'. As Ludmilla Jordanova points out, historical knowledge must be distinguished from other ways of thinking about or describing the past such as myth, tradition and opinion.[7] The crucial feature of historical knowledge is that it is based on evidence.

Although the past is no longer with us and cannot be experienced directly, human existence and action in the past have left physical traces or marks which have survived to the present and which, therefore, we can experience. These are 'sources'. These include such things as physical remains and works of art but the most important are written records. It is the study of these remains that can lead us to knowledge of the past, however tentative. However, this investigation has to be done in a particular way so as to get the most out of the traces of the past and to avoid frequent traps or problems. It is this technique of investigation that forms the core of many courses in historical methodology and is discussed in works such as those of Marwick, Elton, Kitson Clark, Hexter, and many others. The task of the historian, in the empiricist way of thinking, is similar to that of the news reporter or detective – to construct a picture of the past from the indirect or second-hand evidence that is available. The goal of the historical profession as a whole is both to construct and extend this picture of the past and to increase the degree of certainty that can be given to various statements about the past that compose the picture. Clearly, this involves a whole range of skills, techniques and sub-disciplines, including such areas as **palaeography**, **diplomatics** and **philology**.

However, the analogy given above is not a complete one. The aim of the reporter or detective is to provide an accurate account of a particular event. The historian has to do more than this. Historians have to fit the knowledge of the events together to form a larger **narrative**. This is necessary because otherwise it would not be possible to answer crucial questions about the causes of particular events and their relationship to each other. It is at this point that the arguments really begin. Almost all historians accept the argument given above. Even Hayden White, the doyen of postmodernism in history, accepts that we can know and make true statements about events. However, White and many other thinkers argue that once we move from events to larger narratives or analyses we leave behind the world of factual knowledge, however defined.[8] In this view historians put together facts about events to form a narrative and in so doing *create* a meaning. Because of the central role of the actual historian in the creation of this account, the final product is a form of literature and its meaning and truth are dependent upon the position and perspective of the historian who has produced it. This **auteur** theory of historical writing (as Marwick calls it) has many distinguished exponents, including such figures as Collingwood, Croce, Becker, Oakeshott and Lukács.[9] This is not a matter of ideology, as the wide range of political opinions in the list above indicates. It rather reflects a shared theory of knowledge, of epistemology, specifically an **idealist** one, derived ultimately from Plato but developed in the modern world by thinkers such as Kant and Hegel. (In this, as in other respects, Marx's position was complex. He believed that an empirical, scientific history was possible but that most actual historiography was not of this kind because it was produced from a perspective distorted by class position.)

How though does an empiricist historian respond to this challenge? There is evidence from historians' own accounts of their work to support the *auteur* model. For example, the Victorian historian James Anthony Froude remarked in a lecture in 1864: 'It often seems to me as if history is like a child's box of letters, with which we can spell any word we please. We have only to pick out such letters as we want, arrange them as we like, and say nothing about those which do not suit our purpose.'[10] This seems conclusive. However, more thought will show there is a possible response to this.

Historians are confronted by a mass of information, or knowledge of past events, derived from physical sources. They must try to fit this together to form a coherent, larger pattern. So far, Froude is correct. However, they cannot be combined in any way that the historian pleases – in this respect Froude was wrong. This becomes more clear if we change the analogy slightly and think of the known events as being like plastic bricks rather than letters. The 'bricks' can be put together to form structures – the historian does play a crucial role here. However, many combinations are ruled out by the nature and shape of the 'bricks'. So, for example, we could not have an account that violated known **chronology**. Some 'structures' will be able to make use of or incorporate (explain) more 'bricks' than others. Some will be more stable and solid than others, some will have gaps in them. The way certain shaped 'bricks' combine with others will only become clear when they are placed alongside others, or once a 'structure' has been put together. (The full significance if certain facts/events will become apparent only when they are considered not in isolation but in relation to others.) So, to complete the analogy, historians are like children in a vast playroom, surrounded by piles of plastic bricks which they fit together to form shapes (pictures and accounts of the past). To add to their difficulties, many of the bricks are lost or damaged and a conveyor belt is constantly dumping fresh bricks into the room. This means their task is very difficult and requires great attention to detail. It does not mean that it is *theoretically* impossible. Moreover, much can be achieved by co-operation among the historians and by building on and developing the structures put together by earlier occupants of the playroom (that is, previous generations of historians).

What conclusions can we draw from this about empiricist history as a doctrine and a practice? First and foremost, not all interpretations or accounts of the past are equally acceptable: some are ruled out by the empirical evidence, or by the lack of it. Statements about the past can and should only be made if they can be grounded in and defended by reference to material sources. Second, that we can compare different accounts of the past on an empirical basis, that is, on the basis of how far they are consonant with the evidence, and can, if the evidence allows, make judgements on that basis as to which account is 'better'. We do not have to rely only upon judgements of rhetoric, style, or utility for contemporary politics, as the postmodernists would have us believe.[11]

Third, it is possible to amend or improve accounts so that they become more robust and incorporate more events. In other words historical knowledge is *cumulative* and increases as the process of historical investigation continues. The increase takes two forms: a growth in the number of things that are known (of statements that can be made about the past) and of the degree of certainty that can be given to statements about the past. This is why (in most cases) more recent works are to be preferred to older ones, no matter how well written. Fourth, that the process of historical investigation is, in a very real sense, collaborative. This co-operation is achieved by the organization of scholarship through a number of institutions and practices.

Fifth, that the survival of written records is vitally important. This is simply because they contain far more information than other kinds of evidence and therefore allow *less*, not more, scope for the imagination of the historian. This in turn means that much of the past is in practice not accessible to the historian and cannot be the subject of historical investigation. It does not mean, however, that the historian can, or should, confine their attentions to such matters as political history, where records are relatively abundant. Part of the development of empirical history has been the application of its method to areas where records are scarce. However, it remains the case that no sources means no knowledge.

Sixth, that much of the knowledge of the past gained by this method depends upon induction, that is, upon research into particular cases which is then made the basis for generalization. These general hypotheses may in turn lead to further research so that an 'inductive cycle' is set up, but it is the research into specific cases which is the starting point. Finally, the effect of historical research, when conducted in this fashion, is both constructive and destructive. It leads to greater and more surely founded knowledge of the past. However, it also frequently undermines and dissolves beliefs about the past based upon other, less secure foundations, as both Jordanova and Elton have observed. This can be a painful experience. It can also, however, be liberating, not least in the way it destroys myths that maintain existing relations of power in society.

All of this still leaves room for disagreement among historians who accept the empirical basis of their subject and its method. Topics which have often provoked warm disagreement include the question of whether history is an art or a **science**, the issue of whether it has a social purpose or should concern itself solely with the establishing of fact, and the *extent* to which objective judgement is possible as a result of following the correct method (as opposed to its actual possibility).

To return to a point made earlier, however, the beliefs set out above, and the practices which employ them, have not always existed. It may be the case that human beings have always written about the past, but empirical history is a relatively recent development. How then did it come to be?

1 The Creation of Empirical History

▶ Historical writing before the coming of empiricism

People have kept records of the past and written about it since the dawn of civilization. Empirical history, however, is a relatively new development. Like **science**, it is a modern phenomenon and its origins lie in the intellectual ferment and divisions of the early modern period, the age of Renaissance and Reformation. It is important to realize that not all cultures, at all times, think about the past or knowledge of the past in the same way. Europeans in the Middle Ages had a view of the past that was quite different from the one commonly held today. Consequently, the development of the dominant modern concept of history, one founded upon an empirical theory of knowledge, involved a significant rupture or change in the way educated people thought about the past and their relation to it.

Empiricism as a theory of knowledge was known in the Middle Ages. This came mainly from contact with Arab writers rather than directly from its origins in the ancient world. Thinkers such as William of Ockham are usually put in the **epistemological** tradition of empiricism by historians of philosophy and he was indeed responsible for formulating one of the principles of empirical method, the least entity rule, known after him as **'Ockham's Razor'**. However, this kind of thinking had little or no impact on the way medieval writers thought about the past. Their thinking in this area was dominated by the ideas of St Augustine, and in particular his great work *City of God*. From this came the idea of the human past as an unfolding sequential story, which showed the workings in human affairs of divine purpose, the high points of which were Christ's death and resurrection and, as the culmination of the story, his return and the apocalypse. One result of Augustine's influence was the loss of the historical thought of the ancient world, so that the sophisticated cyclical theories of writers such as Polybius were forgotten.

The dominance of this **providential** view of history and the loss of the classical perspective meant that the medieval view of the past was, to our eyes, radically ahistorical. The most dramatic aspect of this was the almost complete lack of a historical sense. That is to say, medieval authors were not aware of the past as something distinct and different from the present, nor did they see the present as the product of a process of historical change. This led to what we would regard as amazing **anachronisms** in the way the past was portrayed. People saw nothing strange in the portrayal of the first-century Roman emperors Vespasian and Titus as Crusaders or in the description of Troy as a walled town with towers and bells, like an Italian city-state, with Hector and Achilles armed and equipped like medieval knights. The emphasis on divine **providence** as the fundamental force in history meant that there was no serious effort at explaining the causation of events: everything could be ultimately accounted for by reference to God's will, which was not yet understood fully by human beings. Moreover, God was seen as intervening and acting directly and constantly in human affairs, through the workings of chance and fortune, and through miraculous events, where the normal rules and expectations that applied to the natural world were suspended.

Closely related to this was the constant use of **arguments from authority**; that is, matters of dispute would be settled not by appeal to empirical investigation or research, but by citing tradition or an author or text held to be authoritative by virtue of their status. The highest authority was, naturally, the Bible, which meant that any historical account or explanation that could be shown to be incompatible with the Biblical text would be rejected out of hand. In general there was no real criticism of **sources** or evaluation of their veracity. Documents originating from hundreds of years after an event were given the same credence as contemporaneous ones. Sources that to the modern eye are clearly fictional or fraudulent, such as the pseudo-Callisthenes account of the life of Alexander, were treated as sober truth. No attempt was made to distinguish between accounts on the grounds of probability – in fact, writers would often include fictional episodes on the grounds that they were a good story or made a moral point, while tales of the miraculous would be included to demonstrate God's role or his favouring of the side taken by the writer.

In general medieval writers did not make the distinction we now draw between fact and fiction. The word 'history' meant simply a story or narrative. Such a story would be true in so far as it was about people who had actually lived, or events that had actually happened, but these were used and woven together with material that was simply invented, to create an account which would be judged on the basis of its internal coherence, attractiveness, or ability to inspire feeling rather than any correspondence with certain knowledge.[1]

▶ The historical revolution and its origins

This began to change in the fifteenth century, under the influence of Renaissance **humanism**, but the real break with the medieval way of thinking, the 'historical revolution', as Fussner calls it, occurred in the sixteenth and seventeenth centuries.[2] Particularly significant were the years between about 1550 and 1650. In those years a change took place in the way the past was conceived of in its relation to the present. This led in turn to a novel kind of study of the past and its records. At the same time new methods were developed for the establishing of knowledge, in history as much as in science. All of this was a slow and erratic process. As with all episodes in history, there is as much continuity as change and many of the intellectual figures of this age are sometimes seen anachronistically as more 'modern' (that is, like ourselves) than they really were. Nevertheless, the view of the past held by an educated person in 1680 was very different from that of his counterpart in 1480 or 1580.

The 'historical revolution' of the early modern period had a number of distinct but related elements. The first was the development of a historical sense, an awareness both that the past was different from the present and that it had to be understood in its own terms. This led to an interest in explaining how it was that the present state of affairs had come about. The second was the development, very tentative at first, of **non-providential** forms of causation or at least of a way of defining providence which put less stress on active divine intervention in human affairs. Along with this went a greater **scepticism** about fantastic or fabulous stories and even, increasingly, about miracles. Third was the increased reliance upon documents and antiquities as sources of information about the past. The last was the development of techniques for the study and analysis of documents and of technical aids such as glossaries, dictionaries and, increasingly, libraries and archives.

The 'historical revolution' was not confined to any one part of Europe but involved figures from Italy, France, Spain, the Empire and England. However, the first signs appeared in Italy. One of the earliest events in the story was the demonstration by Lorenzo Valla that the *Donation of Constantine*, a document that purported to record the granting by the Roman emperor Constantine the Great of temporal powers over a large part of Italy to the Pope, was a forgery from the early Middle Ages. Valla's motives were not scholarly but polemical, as his aim was to embarrass the papacy. The significance of his demonstration lay in the way it was done, by applying critical techniques and particularly linguistic analysis to the text of the *Donation* to demonstrate that it could not possibly have been a product of the fourth century. It was one of the first examples of critical scrutiny and analysis of a documentary source that ignored the claims of authority.[3]

The 'historical revolution' of the sixteenth and seventeenth centuries is itself a historical phenomenon. That is, it was a complex series of related phenomena that occurred during a specific period of the past and which we know about because of the remains or traces it has left. As ever, historians are divided over what its precise cause was. Even so, there is broad agreement on the way that four main features of the political and intellectual history of the time brought about this change, almost as a side-effect.

The earliest was the growth of interest in antiquity, that is, classical Greece and Rome. This was associated with what is commonly known as 'humanism'.

Renaissance humanism was very different from its modern counterpart. It referred to the revival of interest in the fifteenth century in the learning and philosophy of the ancient world, particularly of the Greeks. A central element of this was the attempt to revive the classical curriculum of the 'humane studies' such as rhetoric, poetry and history as opposed to theology, hence 'humanism'. A major aspect of this intellectual movement was an elevating of the antique past and a corresponding disparaging of the more recent past. This had a number of important consequences.

One was the first sign of a historical sense, or historical self-consciousness on the part of educated Europeans. The interest in the ancient world and the contrasts drawn between it and the centuries that had followed, as well as the present, made people more aware of the differences between the present and the past. It also led to an awareness of historical change, due to interest in the decline of classical antiquity and in the way it had been replaced by what was now seen as a quite distinct kind of society. However, this growth in historical awareness went along with a great interest in rhetoric and the style and structure of classical writers such as Cicero, Herodotus and Thucydides. Consequently, there was a deliberate attempt to imitate these models so, initially, the impact of humanism was to reinforce the view of history as a branch of literature. This had reached such a point by the second part of the sixteenth century that some authors, such as Sir Philip Sidney, saw history as simply a special form of fiction, and consigned it to the discipline of poetry.

Another important element of the intellectual climate of the time was the rediscovery of classical sceptical philosophy. This was only one part of the general recovery of classical Greek philosophy that took place in the second half of the fifteenth century. Philosophical traditions such as Stoicism and Epicureanism, which had been forgotten or ignored for most of the medieval period, were rediscovered and became the subjects of warm controversy. Particularly important was the rediscovery of the third-century Greek sceptic philosopher Sextus Empiricus. He was rediscovered in manuscripts brought to Italy after the fall of Constantinople in 1453. A Latin translation of his major work, *Outline of Pyrrhonism*, was published in 1562 and an edition of his complete works in 1569. The ideas of Sextus achieved wide circulation, not least because of their adoption by the famous sixteenth-century French sceptic Michel de Montaigne, most notably in his longest essay, the *Apology for Raymond Sebond*. Sextus, and his followers, argued that the uncertainty of all sources of knowledge meant that nothing could be truly known. (One sceptical work of the sixteenth century was titled *Quod Nihil Scitur*, that is, That Nothing is Known).[4]

To the modern eye these ideas would seem to fit with religious doubt and even disbelief. However, they were largely introduced by religious polemicists as part of the debate between Catholic and Protestant. Sceptical arguments were used both to attack the other side's philosophy and to argue that the inability of reason to establish truth and knowledge left no options except faith, and authority or revealed truth. By 1600, however, religious thinkers had indeed become alarmed by the threat such arguments posed to religious belief.

The challenge of scepticism brought forth a response, in the works of authors such as Francis Bacon. Bacon argued for what would now be called a **fallibilistic** definition of knowledge, that is, while we may not know anything with certainty, we can know things tentatively and can acquire a greater degree of certainty by the process of cumulative **induction** (see above, p. 4). He also argued that, while there are obvious problems with sense-evidence as a source of knowledge, it yielded greater certainty that any other source. This position, of moderate scepticism and reliance upon the evidence of the senses for our knowledge of the world, was the foundation of the later philosophical tradition of 'British empiricism'. In his major work, the *Novum Organum*, Bacon set out a systematic method for investigating the material world and obtaining increasing amounts of more certain knowledge about it.[5]

These philosophical arguments had a direct bearing on thinking about history in at least two ways. The scepticism of Renaissance **Pyrrhonists** such as Montaigne undermined the power of appeals to authority or **intuition** as sources of knowledge and made writers more sceptical about fantastic claims or stories. The response, founding knowledge on sense experience but nothing else, led to the appearance of systematic methods of inquiry, in history as much as in science.

The factor that played the greatest role in the emergence of a new historical thought and practice, however, was religious and political conflict. The period of the 'historical revolution' was also the age both of Reformation and Counter-Reformation and the rise of the modern state. Both of these were a spur to historical inquiry, of a kind that had not existed before. Protestantism was by its nature interested in both the history of the early Church, to which it claimed it was returning, and the process by which 'corruptions' had come about in doctrine and practice. This naturally provoked a Catholic response, seeking to attack the claims of reformers and defend the medieval Church. Both sides of the argument were therefore very interested in the history of the Church as an institution. A frantic search for precedents was a significant part of the conflict in all parts of Europe. Henry VIII, for example, used several historically based arguments to support his claims to royal supremacy and for England's status as an 'empire', that is, a separate, independent state.

The sixteenth century also saw a change in the nature of warfare, and consequently a transformation in both the theory and practice of government. In most parts of Europe rulers expanded their power, developed a new kind of administration, and sought to defend this by appeal to the new doctrine of what came to be called 'sovereignty'. This provoked strong, often violent resistance, even armed rebellion, from the interests and institutions threatened by these new developments. Again both sides were interested in appealing to the past to gain support for their position, but this was particularly true of those who sought to resist the innovations of reforming monarchs. Since these reforms tended to undermine the position of older legal and representative institutions, there was a growing interest in the past history of those institutions. The intention was to produce an account that would show that rebels were in fact upholding an old, established order against wrongful innovation, and providing authority from the past for actions taken in the present. Rulers for their part were equally swift to resort to this search for historical origins and precedent. All of this conflict led to a growth of interest in the past and the history of law, government and institutions. This can be seen very clearly in the Dutch Revolts of 1567 onwards and in France during the religious wars after 1559. To give just one of many examples, the *Francogallia* of François Hotman was a justification of resistance, which consisted primarily of a constitutional history of the French monarchy. In England during the Civil War, both King and Parliament tried to base their arguments on historical precedent, with Denzil Holles becoming a kind of '**antiquarian** in chief' for the Parliamentary cause.[6]

The last factor to consider was the so-called 'reception' of Roman law during the sixteenth and early seventeenth centuries. Roman law had been known and studied in Western Europe since the discovery of the *Corpus Juriis Civilis* of Justinian in the eleventh century. However, the medieval approach to Roman law was, like so much else, completely ahistorical, with no awareness of the many differences between Roman and medieval society. Instead, the contents of the *Corpus* were twisted and glossed to make them fit contemporary circumstances, with no real understanding of what the historical meaning of the text actually was. One part of the growth of modern government was the replacement of traditional, customary law by a system based upon Roman law, this process being known as the 'reception' of Roman law. This led to the growth of a historical jurisprudence in which scholars sought to recover the original content and meaning of the original Roman texts. The *Corpus* was no longer seen as a work of timeless philosophy (the characteristic medieval approach), but as a kind of relic or monument of the classical world, in much the same way as an aqueduct or the Coliseum. As the classical world was seen as superior to the present, it became the task of scholars to uncover from this monument the principles of Roman law as they had been, so that they could be reapplied in the present. So, the result was the historical study of law and the development of a range of techniques for understanding legal documents, particularly **diplomatics** and **philology**.[7]

We can see how the four factors just set out combined together to bring about a change in the way people thought about the past. Renaissance humanism with its cult of antiquity brought the first awareness of a difference between past and present and led to a new interest in Roman legal history. This in turn produced new techniques for the analysis of records. At the same time innovations by rulers and religious disputes brought about an interest in recovering the past of institutions.

This meant much more use of the documentary and other records left by those institutions, which were analysed using the techniques developed by legal scholars. There was also the rise of a new way of thinking about knowledge and investigation derived from the impact of sceptical philosophy. This was initially used as a weapon in religious and political disputes, and had its origin in the Renaissance fascination with classical antiquity.

▶ The course and growth of the 'historical revolution'

So the factors which produced the change were mutually reinforcing. The humanist scholarship of the fifteenth century and the work of men like Valla led to an intense interest in words and language, particularly in the meaning of words and the way that words acquired meaning. The study of such topics was given a new name, that of philology. This involved the study of texts and the use of words or expressions in those texts so as to establish the meaning of the words or expressions. This was defined in terms of the 'thing' to which the words referred, their **referent**. The scholars soon realised that this often depended upon the context, both in the sense of the surrounding words and that of the physical and historical context in which the text had been produced. They became particularly interested in the origins of words, their **etymology**, and in the way their meaning changed over time and between places. As well as textual criticism, a number of other technical disciplines came into being. These included **numismatics**, the study of coins; **epigraphy**, the study of inscriptions; and **palaeography**, the study of the actual physical manuscript or medium and the handwriting on it. The most important was diplomatics, the technical study of documents, which by examining such matters as the style, language, technical usages and structure of texts could establish their authenticity, origin and status (that is, whether they were a copy or an original).

Legal history was the first area where new historical methods took root. The use of new methods and their application to legal texts led to the appearance of the historical school of **jurisprudence**, that is, a body of thinkers who saw law not in terms of timeless philosophy, but as an historical phenomenon. This school of thought had an impact in several parts of Europe but it was France where it had the greatest effect. The founding figure was Guillaume Bude (1468–1540), who taught at the law school at Orleans and introduced humanist scholarship into France. He was one of the first people outside Italy to apply the new methods to the *Corpus* and in particular the *Digest* (the part of the *Corpus* where Justinian's compilers put together examples of Roman case law). He established that Roman law as found in the *Corpus* was not a complete system based on first principles, but the end product of a long process of social change, in the course of which many terms had changed their meaning. He had several pupils who built on his work, the most significant being Louis LeRoy (1510–1577). He was as responsible as anyone for developing the notion of historical **relativism**, that is, the idea that historical periods and figures had to be judged on their own terms and not on the basis of anachronistic, present-derived values.

The next major figure, however, was Andrea Alciato (1492–1550), who, although an Italian and graduate of Bologna, spent most of his career at Bourges in France. He introduced philology and historical analysis into the teaching of law. More important for our interests, he set in train the historical study of law as an institution, which led by extension to the historical study of other institutions associated with the law, such as parliaments. The generation that succeeded his had a number of important historical legists among its members. The most important were François Baudoin (1520–1573) and Jean Bodin (1530–1596). These were the two who defined for later generations the content and methods of the emerging discipline.[8]

► The definition of empirical method

The intellectual context for this was the impact of Pyrrhonism. By the 1580s this had had a substantial impact on contemporary thinking. It led to a sharp critique of the emerging discipline of history, one very similar in fact to the contemporary assault from postmodernists. Then, as now, it was philosophers and literary figures who led the assault. For authors such as Sir Philip Sidney, history claimed a degree of knowledge that it did not have, and was no more that a subordinate branch of rhetoric or poetry with ideas above its station. Baudoin and Bodin rebutted these charges by defining what the scope and nature of historical study was and by clearly setting out the method to be followed. They did this by turning the methods developed by legal historians such as Alciato into a more general methodology for investigating the past. The works in which they did this were *The Institution of Universal History* (Baudoin), published in 1561, and *Method for Easily Understanding History* (Bodin), published in 1566.[9]

Bodin's work in particular was a highly organized, systematic treatise or handbook on how to conduct historical research, the first of many such works.[10] Baudoin's work was a more philosophical one, concerned more with the scope and content of history. Both contained elements that would surprise a modern reader, such as the emphasis in Bodin on such occult disciplines as astrology and numerology. Both works, however, had a number of common features and in response to Pyrrhonism articulated for the first time an empiricist model of gaining knowledge of the past. They argued that the physical products or remains of the past, such as documents, monuments and artefacts, were part of the past and so their study enabled the present-day student to recover knowledge of the otherwise inaccessible past. They made the explicit distinction, now a cornerstone of historical analysis, between original or **primary sources** and **secondary** writings, and emphasized the primacy of the former. Both set out the methods that could be used to establish the authenticity of sources and to clarify their meaning. Bodin in particular set out how the historian had to approach all evidence in a way that was cautious and sceptical, aware always of the potential partiality and bias of the writer of the source.

The aim of this critical approach to sources was not, however, as it was with the Pyrrhonists, to cast doubt on the very idea of knowledge, but rather to ensure that the historian could be as sure as possible about the truth of his statements. Scepticism was made a method for testing statements so as to eliminate the untrue or highly doubtful and leave only the more reliable. Baudoin defined the scope of history as being the totality of the human past, as distinct from the natural history of the world, which dealt with such matters as zoology and the material world. This meant, as Bodin also argued, that history was ideally not confined to the study of any one aspect of human activity, or of one part of the world.

One striking feature of the thought of both men was their emphasis on the utility of historical study as a guide to present action. Bodin in particular saw history as the most essential element in the education of statesmen and argued that history was in some ways the foundational discipline on which others were built. This emphasis reflected the times in which both men lived and their view of them. Both belonged to the 'politique' group in French politics, who sought a compromise between the Protestant and Catholic factions whose struggles had plunged France into decades of savage civil war. (Baudoin had earlier been a Calvinist but had moved away from this position.) One of the purposes of correct historical inquiry for both men was to provide a disinterested historical knowledge, which would free men from the distorted views of furious partisans.

▶ The rise of empirical antiquarianism

The desire of partisans to find historical precedents for their cause and the development of critical techniques by the legal scholars bore fruit in the growth of systematic **antiquarianism**, in England as much as in France or Germany. The driving force behind much of this was **chorography**, that is, the attempt to recover as much knowledge as possible about the past of a particular place or geographical area. This was the work of antiquaries or, to use the French term that was increasingly used to describe them, the *erudits*. The aim of antiquarianism was to collect as much factual information as possible about a topic, usually a location, so as to produce a picture, or series of pictures, of the past. This involved the use of accurate and detailed citation of the source of the information. Sometimes antiquarian investigation could be politically controversial, as for example in the work of the French author Jacques-Auguste De Thou (1553–1617), who managed to offend both the Catholic church (despite being a Catholic himself, his works were placed on the *Index* of prohibited books) and King James I, who took exception to his account of his mother's reign.

In England there were a number of antiquarians who produced important works. Perhaps the most notable was William Camden (1551–1623), who in his *Britannia* presented for the first time a compilation of all that was then known about Roman Britain. Others were John Stow (1525–1605) and John Selden (1584–1645). One of the most important continental figures was Josef Justus Scaliger (1540–1609), who did a great deal for the technical and highly demanding subject of chronology. Stow's work, *Survey of London* (in 1598), effectively created the sub-discipline of local history in England and is still the principal source for Elizabethan and Jacobean London.

John Selden, an important figure in the politics of the early seventeenth century, was primarily responsible for creating another distinct form of antiquarian investigation, that of institutions rather than places. His main historical work was the *Historie of Tithes*, in which he traced the origin and development of that form of taxation. (This fell into the category mentioned earlier, of controversial works.) The other person who played a significant role in developing institutional history was Selden's near contemporary Sir Henry Spelman, who introduced the concept of 'feudalism' into the study of medieval England and its law.

Antiquarianism also led to another development of great importance for historians, the creation by antiquarian book collectors of libraries for research. The most important collectors in England were Matthew Parker (who was Archbishop of Canterbury, 1559–75) and the great Jacobean bibliophile Sir Robert Cotton. Cotton's library, in particular, preserved large numbers of medieval manuscripts and Tudor state papers and made possible much of the research of antiquaries such as Spelman and Selden. Later on Robert Harley created another great collection through the agency of his librarian Humphrey Wanley. (The Cottonian and Harleian libraries, together with the Royal library, formed the basis of the British Museum library.) On the other hand, archives and government papers were still hopelessly disorganized, where they existed at all, and systematic collection and sorting of records in archives had to wait until the nineteenth century.[11]

The process of antiquarian research or 'erudition' as it came to be known, continued throughout the seventeenth century and into the eighteenth. These dedicated researchers built on the methodological foundations of writers such as Baudoin and Bodin and established many of the conventions of modern scholarship such as the **citation** of sources through the footnote, the list of sources and works consulted in the bibliography, and the critical analysis of original documents as the best (or least doubtful) source of knowledge. Much of the most important work was carried out by the ecclesiastical historians associated with the Congregation of St Maur, based at St Germain des Pres in Paris, of whom the best known was

Jean Mabillon (1632–1707). It was he and the other **Maurists** who brought diplomatics and palaeography to the highest level they had yet attained. In the process they discredited many legends and traditions and exposed many ecclesiastical documents as forgeries. The culmination of this *erudit* tradition was perhaps the work of the Italian author Ludovico-Antonio Muratori (1672–1750). His two major works were the 25 volumes of the *Rerum Italicarum Scriptores* (1723–51) and the six-volume *Antiquitates Italiae medii aevi* (1738–42). In the first he produced a printed edition of an enormous mass of chronicles and other primary materials. In the second he put together no less than 75 dissertations on a range of topics in medieval Italian history, in which he compiled all that could be known about them from the original sources.[12]

▶ Speculative history and the Enlightenment response to antiquarianism

The achievements of the *erudits* were thus considerable and historians still draw on them today (for example Muratori's edition of medieval primary sources has still not been replaced). However, there were substantial limitations to their work. One was the persistence of providential models of historical causation well into the eighteenth century and beyond, which hampered the search for other forms of explanation. Another was that documentary analysis was still often uncritical. A practical difficulty was the difficulty of access to many original sources, which still lay piled up, unsorted and filthy in official depositories. The major limitation, however, was the lack of **narrative**, which meant that antiquarian works were long on description but short on explanation. The work of *erudits* came to be seen as nothing more than the piling up of a mountain of disconnected and hence ultimately useless **facts**. At the same time many of the controversies and intellectual movements which had provided the original impetus to the movement had died away by the early eighteenth century. The stage was now set for a new departure in **historiography**, which was in some ways a reaction against the empiricism of the *erudits* but eventually came to complement it.

This departure was 'speculative' history, which became a major feature of the intellectual movement of the **Enlightenment**. These were large-scale accounts of the history of the world or some large part of it, or of some significant feature of human life. They were driven in the first instance not by the empirical facts of the *erudits*, but by **theories** or abstract models, of the past and of human nature. Their central feature, however, as compared to the antiquarian works of the *erudits*, was narrative. Throughout the seventeenth and eighteenth centuries authors had continued to write narrative histories. There was little or no overlap in personnel, however, between them and the erudite antiquarians. Rather, the two forms of historical investigation continued in parallel. These narrative works did indeed belong to the category of literature as much as history. The best, such as the *History of the Great Rebellion* by Edward Hyde, Earl of Clarendon (1609–1674), and the *History of His Own Time* by Bishop Gilbert Burnet, (1643–1715), dealt with contemporary or near contemporary events. That is, they were concerned with events that had happened in the lifetime or near lifetime of the author. Consequently, they were based largely on personal knowledge and memory or oral testimony rather than documentary research. When they ventured away from matters of living memory, they became much less reliable.[13]

What happened in the eighteenth century was twofold. First, the literary genre of narrative history became much more diverse and varied, moving away from its original topic of political and religious events to deal with a wide range of subjects, the entire past of human experience in fact. This both reflected and in turn reinforced the second phenomenon, the impact on narrative history of the interests and concerns of eighteenth-century intellectuals or, as we would now say, of the Enlightenment. It was this combination that produced the 'speculative history'.[14]

One of the key concepts for European thought from the early eighteenth century onwards was that of 'civilization'. This was effectively a way of thinking about the emerging European society of the time that distinguished it both from the European past and that of the rest of the planet. An essential element was the belief that civilization, defined as a way of living and behaving, had emerged in Europe and was continuing to develop there and to spread to other parts of the world. In other words, it was a historical phenomenon or set of phenomena, including such matters as politics and government, law, the economy and manners or customs. It was associated with another commonplace idea of the time, that there was a common or universal human nature that underlay the apparent diversity of human societies. As David Hume put it: 'Men are much the same in all times and places.' All this led to a great interest in the nature and content of civilization, in its distinction from its opposite, that is savagery or barbarism, and the way it had come about in various parts of the world before reaching its highest point yet (it was thought) in Europe. One result was that Europeans became much more self-conscious (or reflexive as we would now say) about the distinctive features of their own society, both good and bad. This found expression in works such as Montesquieu's *Persian Letters*, an early example of what became a common genre of eighteenth-century literature. This was the 'traveller's report', in which a visitor from a non-European culture would give an account of European ways, usually in a critical manner. In reality of course the author was a European, and the perspective from which the account and criticisms were made was that of a European intellectual, not a genuine outsider.

The other genre produced were the large-scale narrative accounts mentioned above. In these the authors sought to explain how the present (civilized) way of life had come about and also how, in earlier periods, civilization had perished. They were based not on empirical research but on theories: theories of human nature, motivation and psychology, of the role and impact of factors such as geography, religious belief and wealth on human beings and society, and of the overall shape and pattern of world history. They used and employed empirical facts, but this came after the theory.

Montesquieu was one of the earliest and most influential of these writers. His work *The Causes of the Greatness and Decadence of the Romans*, published in 1734, was an early attempt to produce an account not only of political but of intellectual, cultural and social history. He emphasized the role in historical events of impersonal, structural factors such as climate, geography and social and political institutions. In 1756 Voltaire produced one of the first attempts at a comparative cultural history in *An Essay on the Manners and Spirit of the Nations*. These two literary works established a model, which many others followed. One important figure was the Scottish historian William Robertson (1721–1793), who produced four significant works between 1759 and 1791. Robertson's goal was to write primarily political history, which would, however, take account of, and incorporate, social and cultural developments.

A similar approach, in some ways, was taken by David Hume. Today Hume is known as a philosopher, one of the greatest in fact, but his contemporary reputation (and most of his income) depended on his *History of England*. Hume wrote this work in part to attack the domination, as he saw it, of historical argument by one party, that is, the **Whigs**. He began by writing a history of the seventeenth century and then worked backward until the end product was a history from Roman times until 1688. Hume used the information and sources which had been put together by the antiquarians, but did no original research himself. For his account of the events of 1637–88, he depended upon contemporary accounts such as those of Burnet and Clarendon. The principal effect of his work (apart from undermining the traditional Whig view as he had intended) was to spread his own hostile view of religious enthusiasm.[15]

One of the growing interests of eighteenth-century thinkers was the part played in the growth of civilization by trade and commerce. There were several extensive surveys produced, of which the most notable was the *Historical and Chronological Deduction of the Origin of Commerce* (1764) by Adam Anderson. The best known such work by far, however, was of course Adam Smith's *Wealth of Nations* from 1776. Today this book is conventionally seen as the founding text of economics, but it is as much a work of history. A large part of it is an elaborate account of historical development, built around a **stadial** model of history, in which societies pass through a succession of types of economic organization, each with its own distinctive type of social and political order. The last and 'highest' was what Smith called 'commercial society', the emerging society of his own time. This idea had partly come from Robertson, in particular from the *Introductory Essay* to his *History of the Reign of the Emperor Charles V* (1769).

The Scots also got involved in the history of culture and social institutions. The two central figures here were Adam Ferguson and Henry Home, Lord Kames. Ferguson's *History of the Origin and Progress of Civil Society* (1765) is a work that, like Smith's, has been claimed as a founding text by another discipline, in this case sociology. Kames produced several important works in a range of disciplines but his principal historical work was his *Sketches of the History of Man*, which examined what a later author would call the 'civilizing process'.[16]

The other area of speculative history was the history of institutions, whether political, economic or social. Here again, authors drew on the work of the *erudits* but used it to support an analysis based on theory. The most interesting and profound works of institutional 'speculative history' were those of John Millar. In *Origin of the Distinction of Ranks* (1771), he gave a historical account of the nature, origin and development through time of class divisions. In *An Historical View of the English Government*, he produced an analysis of the historical evolution of government in England which related it to economic and social organization.[17]

As we shall see in Chapter 2, eighteenth-century narrative histories are part of the ancestry not only of history, but also of economics, sociology, psychology and anthropology. The authors of this period employed the theories circulating at that time to produce narratives in which they speculated as to the origins and development of political orders, economic organization, ideas and beliefs, and culture and ways of life. Much of this subject matter had been lacking in the work of the antiquarian *erudits*. The new genres of historical writing also gave an order to the factual information accumulated by the *erudits* by using it to support or illustrate a narrative account. However, as noted earlier, it was the theory that was the origin and determinant of this process. The facts were mined to support the theory, rather than being the starting point.

▶ The combination of speculative history and antiquarianism

As we shall see later (Chapter 2 below), the late eighteenth and early nineteenth centuries saw a strong reaction against the theoretical and **universalist** approach of the Enlightenment authors. At the same time something highly significant took place for the story of empirical historical research. This was the merging of the two types of history, the antiquarianism of the *erudits* and the speculative narratives of the *auteurs*, to produce what are recognizably historical works of the modern kind, based upon original research and using the techniques pioneered by the antiquarians, but deploying the results in an extensive narrative of the kind found in the works of Voltaire or Smith.

The best known work of this kind is undoubtedly Gibbon's *Decline and Fall of the Roman Empire*. This is still read with enormous enjoyment today, principally as a work of literature and in no small measure because of Gibbon's acute sense of irony – as one author says, there are many passages in Gibbon which can still make most readers laugh out loud.[18] However, this should not obscure its status as a work of history. It was based on intensive use of all of the sources then available, which Gibbon consulted himself rather than relying on summaries or secondary writings. He provided citations for his assertions, arguments and factual statements, so that readers who disagreed with him (of which there were a fair number) could check the source to see if Gibbon's reading of it was correct or plausible. The book is an enormous compendium of learning, containing most of what was known at that time about such matters as the political and military history of the later Roman Empire, the growth of Christianity, and the incursion of Germanic tribes into the Roman world. However, these facts are woven together to form a narrative with a twofold theme: in Gibbon's own words 'the triumph of barbarism and religion'. These themes give meaning and order to facts that would otherwise remain merely antiquarian curiosities.[19]

By the end of the eighteenth century the principal elements of empirical history had come into being, both as theory and practice. These were the awareness of the distinction between the present and the past and of the reality of historical change; a particular theory of human knowledge in general, that it derived from experience; the principle that true or reliable knowledge of the past could come only from the remains of the past; an understanding of the distinction between primary and secondary sources and of the primacy of the former; technical methods for subjecting sources to critical analysis; and the use of narrative as a means of ordering facts into coherent structures which provided explanation for the causation of particular acts. However, while the elements of empirical history had come into being by 1800, history as it now is – that is, a formal academic discipline – had not (the same could be said of, for example, chemistry or economics). Although Scotland and France had led the way in the eighteenth century, it was in Germany that the practice of empirical history was to be institutionalized and perfected.

2 The Perfection of Empirical History

▶ Difficulties and problems

By the early nineteenth century the elements of empirical history had come into being, but they had not yet come together. There was historical scholarship and there were historians, but history as a discipline, as we understand it today, did not exist. Despite the work of scholars such as Gibbon, much of what was written still belonged to the realm of *belles lettres* rather than what would now be recognized as serious scholarship. To put it another way, the study of history was still dominated by talented amateurs rather than professionals. This situation was not unique to history. Exactly the same point could be made about most of the natural and applied **sciences**, while such disciplines as economics, sociology and psychology had hardly come into existence – they were in a position like that of history during the Renaissance. In fact, only a few academic subjects existed as scholarly disciplines in the modern sense, principally law, theology and philosophy.

The change which took place in the course of the nineteenth century, in history as much as other areas of academic inquiry, was the creation of an institutional form of organization for the subject, so that individual scholars worked within an organized structure with other scholars rather than as isolated *savants*. This was only one aspect of the wider phenomenon of the rise of institutions, which was such a prominent feature of nineteenth-century life in general. It was in Germany that this development of institutions first happened, in intellectual life as much as in commerce.

In his work on nineteenth-century historiography published in 1913, G. P. Gooch identified four problems for historical writing in the early years of the nineteenth century. Most subsequent authors have agreed with his assessment.[1] Two of the difficulties he described have already been mentioned. The first was the long-standing one of difficulty of access to documents and original sources. As well as problems mentioned in the previous chapter, such as the lack of organized archives or of critical editions of **primary sources**, there were other problems of a more political nature. Many rulers were reluctant to give access to their records to people not under their control. Moreover, censorship was widely practised in most European states, while the Catholic Church still enforced the *Index* of prohibited books. Historical research was often politically sensitive and dangerous for those engaged in it.

Gooch also identified a continuing problem of a lack of critical faculty in dealing with sources. Here there was a continuing pattern of excessive **scepticism** on the part of a minority of authors and uncritical credulity by the majority. Gooch mentions by way of example the way that French historians still used the largely mythical accounts of Pharamond as though it was a reliable source, and did not distinguish between sources of differing reliability. The work of scholars such as the **Maurists** had gone a long way to resolving this but it still persisted, particularly among the more literary **narrative** historians.

This was partly because of the most important of the four problems. This was the lack of formal teaching of history, particularly at university level, and the corresponding lack of a formal career structure for historians. Consequently, historians such as Gibbon worked as individuals rather than as members of an organized community of scholars. The important consequence for writing and research was the absence of the system of scholarly checks and mutual support, which are, as we shall see, a crucial part of the actual process of academic investigation.

The final problem was the side-effects of the **rationalism** and **universalism** of the **Enlightenment**. In the previous chapter we saw how the concerns of Enlightenment thought led to a more diverse subject matter for narrative history and so created accounts that made sense of the facts accumulated by the *erudits*. However, this process also had negative results. It made for a strong tendency to view and judge the past from the standpoint of the present, with all the dangers of **anachronism** that entailed. It also led to a tendency to see the course of history as moving towards a predestined end, with the historian's job that of explicating and clarifying the way this process had happened. For Gooch, and other later commentators, another consequence was a lack of interest in the medieval period, seen as a barbarous interlude between two civilizations, but if so, this was soon to change.

One feature of intellectual life that had severely handicapped historical investigation before the Enlightenment was the continuing influence of the idea of divine **providence** as the dominant force in history. Related to this was the persistent notion of the reality of the miraculous, that is, the real existence of events which violated the known laws of nature and could be explained only by reference to an act of divine intervention in earthly affairs. Both of these ideas underwent a pronounced decline during the later eighteenth and early nineteenth centuries, so easing the emergence of the modern type of historical inquiry. A landmark in this process was the publication in 1779 of David Hume's *Dialogues Concerning Natural Religion*. This argued *inter alia* that we should always discount testimony for miraculous events, since the suspension of a natural law is inherently less probable than other explanations such as human error. The idea of providence was undermined both by the success of science in providing explanations for natural phenomena and the ability of authors such as Adam Smith to produce explanations of human social organization based on purely naturalistic assumptions. The decline of the notions of the providential and the miraculous was an enormously significant event in the intellectual history of Europe, with wide implications. For historians, it meant that even individual historians who had strong religious beliefs (as many did) would seek to explain historical change by reference to natural causes and other events within history rather than a divine purpose. This made the systematic search for the causation of historical events possible. Providentialism, however, was very hardy and a large part of the intellectual history of the last 200 years, in history and elsewhere, is best understood as a search for a natural or non-theistic alternative to the old idea of providence.

▶ Ranke and his work

The start of modern empirical historiography in Germany is often dated to 1810. In that year the Danish scholar Barthold Georg Niebuhr (1776–1831) started teaching at the recently reformed University of Berlin. In his lectures on Roman history Niebuhr subjected the sources, most especially the work of the classical writer Livy, to the kind of systematic analysis developed by legal scholars. He was able to show that much of the accepted account of early Roman history in particular was almost entirely legendary, and exposed many faults in Livy's work.

However, Niebuhr was more of a transitional figure, one who applied analysis to teaching and narrative. The real breakthrough, if it can be given a definite date, came in 1824. That year saw the appearance of the first major work by the man who more than anyone else was the founding father of empirical **historiography**. That was of course Leopold von Ranke.[2] To say that Ranke built on the work of people like Gibbon and Niebuhr to produce a truly empirical methodology for historical investigation has become a cliché. Certainly, he was only one of a number of scholars who played their part in this process and some accounts do exaggerate his role. However, the part he played was greater than that of anyone else and was recognized as such by his contemporaries. That something is a cliché does not make it untrue: on the contrary, it is precisely its truth which leads to the repetition that gives it the status of a cliché.

In 1824 Ranke, a young man of 29, published *The History of the Latin and Teutonic Nations*. By his own account he was moved to do this by reading the contemporary accounts of fifteenth- and sixteenth-century Italian history and discovering that these contradicted each other directly and could not be simply reconciled. The resulting work was, by the standards of his later output, not especially impressive. It remains famous because of the Preface in which the young Ranke set out his vision of the goal of the historian. In the well-known, much-quoted passage he declared:

History has had assigned to it the task of judging the past, of instructing the present for the benefit of the ages to come. To such lofty functions this work does not aspire. Its aim is merely to show what actually occurred (*Er will bloss zeigen wie es eigentlich gewesen*).[3]

These apparently simple words have attracted as much attention and detailed analysis as a text in scripture. However, the appendix to the book itself, and Ranke's later writings, makes his meaning quite clear. Ranke put forward, largely by example, a set of practices which the historian should follow in trying to establish knowledge about the past. Some of these can be found in the earlier works of men such as Bodin and Baudoin, but it was Ranke who first applied all of them.

The foundational **premiss** was the empirical principle that as knowledge comes only from experience, knowledge of the past comes from our indirect experience of it via the sources, that is, the physical remains of the past. This meant that a work of history should contain only what could be found in the sources. Any assertion or 'truth statement' should be capable of being supported by reference to a source if challenged. This meant that there was no room for imagination or **intuition**, or for statements based on feeling or an *a priori* theory, such as a doctrine about human nature. Late in his life Ranke described how as a young man, after reading Walter Scott's *Quentin Durward*, he then read the memoirs of Philippe de Commines and discovered that the imaginative portrayal of Charles the Bold and Louis XI by Scott bore no relation to the one given by their contemporaries. As he put it: 'I found by comparison that the truth was more interesting and beautiful than the romance. I turned away from it and resolved to avoid all invention and imagination in my works and to stick to facts.'[4]

This episode also reveals one of the principles which Ranke established, that of the hierarchy of sources. Simply, not all were of equal value. The first rule for sorting sources into the more and less valuable was that those closer to the event should be valued more highly and given greater credence. This meant, first, that sources which were contemporaneous with the events they described (primary sources) had a greater value than later writings (**secondary sources**). It also meant that sources produced by the actual actors or direct observers of events were to be preferred to ones produced by commentators or indirect observers, even if they were produced at the same time. This made the precise dating of sources a matter of vital importance.

Ranke also argued for a particular way of reading and analysing sources. This drew on the work of the *erudits*, going back to authors like Bodin, but was more systematic. As well as using the techniques of **philology** to analyse the internal meaning of texts and to date them, the historian had to put a series of tests or questions to the evidence of the text. These included the aim or purpose for which it was produced, its intended audience, the context in which it was produced and, above all, the nature, aims, interests and inclinations of the author. Contemporary handbooks for students of history, such as those of Hexter, Kitson Clark and Marwick, often set out the questions or inquiries which the historian has to make of their sources.[5] It is the degree to which these can be answered which, together with the actual availability of sources, determines the degree of certainty with which statements about past events can be made.

This leads to another principle which Ranke emphasized, that of **citation** of evidence. He stated in his introduction that all of the assertions he made would be supported by a full citation of the source on which it was based, with the citation on the same page as the assertion. Here he was following the practice already established by Gibbon and others, of footnoting authorities for one's account or description, but he also took it further. The new element was the citation in detail of the primary sources, as well as the printed authorities. This was (and is) enormously important. The point of the citation was that any reader could follow the 'directions' given in the footnote to the *precise* source for the statement being made. They could then judge for themselves whether the statement was justified. This was one of the things that made it possible for scholars to check each other and to correct their mistakes or misinterpretations, an essential element of the cumulative growth of knowledge. It also had the effect of preventing fraud or incompetence. The practice of supporting assertions with citations of the evidence for them also revealed to the reader which assertions could be supported in this way and those which could not. This laid bare to the reader those parts of a work which were based on assumption or **theory** rather than empirical investigation.

One argument, which Ranke explicitly made in the famous quote given above, was that historians should avoid judgement of the past in terms of the present. In other words, the historian should not judge people in the past by the standards of the present day or impute motives to them which would make sense for the historian's own time, but not for the time they were writing about. In other words, the great sin to avoid was that of anachronism, of reading present-day concerns, beliefs and ideas into the past. The trap to avoid was **presentism**, meaning a study of the past that was driven by the active issues and debates of the historian's own time. As Ranke said, this also meant that historians were not in the business of providing moral lessons or guidance for the present or the future. Their job was simply to find out as much as possible about the past itself, on its own terms.

This reflects another key idea developed by Ranke and other nineteenth-century German scholars. This was that the past had its own nature, which was distinct from the present. Although there were some generalizations that could be made about all human beings in all times and places, these were commonplaces which, while true, were essentially trivial. Each historical time and place had its own nature, which it was the task of the historian to uncover and understand. (This meant, among other things, understanding how words and language had been used and how this differed from the usage of the historian's own time.) The key to understanding a historical period or place was the '**Zeitgeist**' or 'spirit of the age', meaning the assumptions and basic, unquestioned beliefs of the time. The implication is that each age has unique qualities and values of its own. This means that in some senses, separate historical periods are **incommensurable** because they have different essences or identities.

This would seem to make long-term history impossible. If each age can be understood only on its own terms, we must surely end up with a set of distinct histories, each concerned with one period or age. The answer for empirical historians since Ranke is twofold. First, history as an enterprise has modest goals. Its aim is simply to find out what happened, rather than to establish general or universal principles. The really important answer to this problem, however, is the nature of historical causation. The arrow of historical causation runs from past to present, just as in the physical world which we perceive. So, it is the past that determines the present, not the other way round. The past is in turn determined by the more distant past, and so on. This means that each age both shapes the one that follows it and is itself shaped by the one which preceded it. So it is possible to write a history in which each age is looked at on its own terms, but that nature is explained partly by what has gone before: *not*, however, by what comes after.

This set of ideas came to be known in German as '*historismus*', usually translated in English as '**historicism**'.[6] It makes history the master discipline of the humanities and social sciences because it means that the present can only be fully understood by reference to the past. For Ranke, and most empirical historians since then, it also means that the past cannot be understood in **teleological** terms, as movement towards a definite goal or end state. Ultimate purpose or ends are not part of the historian's concerns. So Ranke, although a devout Christian, did not believe the historian could make any claims to understand God's purpose or to use providence as a way of explaining historical events – even the rise of Christianity itself. Towards the end of his life, in his *Universal History* he remarked:

> In pronouncing the name of Jesus Christ, though I am a good evangelical Christian, I must decline to discuss the religious secret which, being incomprehensible, is beyond the grasp of history. Of God the Son I can speak as little as of God the Father. The historian can only show the combination of world-historic influences in which Christianity appeared and by which its operation was conditioned.[7]

Again, as Gooch pointed out, 'he [Ranke] declared it impossible to prove a directing will leading mankind from point to point or an immanent force driving him towards a goal.'[8] As we shall see, this is one of the areas where empirical history has been most subject to criticism, from Ranke's time onwards.

Another central notion that Ranke formulated was the primacy of **facts**, meaning **truth statements** founded on evidence that was relatively certain. **Hypotheses** had to give way when confronted by facts that contradicted their premises.

Moreover, the establishing of facts had to come first, before the formulation of explanatory hypotheses. These could then lead to further investigation which would uncover more facts, but the facts had to be the starting point. As Richard Evans has pointed out, this has important implications for the way research is done. Historians must not trawl through sources looking for facts that support or confirm a hypothesis. Instead, they should seek to test it by looking for evidence that would disprove it.[9] The reality is that often the investigator has only a vague or unformulated hypothesis and the facts uncovered in the research cause them to amend or refine it and give it clearer definition, before returning to the research. What are to be avoided at all costs, from this perspective, are 'open-ended' theories that have the quality of being so elastic that they can incorporate *any* fact, so that they cannot be disproved.

The final element of empirical history that we can trace to Ranke and his contemporaries is the application of **nominalism** to historical reasoning. Nominalism is a philosophical tradition that can be traced back to the Middle Ages and thinkers such as William of Ockham. It holds that 'universals' (that is, words such as 'mountain', 'cat', or 'man', which refer not to particular cases but an entire class of entities) do not have a real existence, but are simply names or labels of convenience, given because observation tells us that a number of particular entities have certain features in common. Applied to history, this means that terms such as 'feudalism' and 'capitalism' have no real existence, that is, they do not refer to any actual concrete entity that can be perceived by the senses. Rather, they are a label or category, created by the historian to make it easier to understand and talk about many distinct individual instances of such social relations as landholding for which we have evidence, and which share certain common features. So, general terms are analytical tools rather than real entities. This means that in research and writing the specific and particular is often emphasized at the expense of the general (the focus is often on the trees rather than the wood).

▶ The growth of professional history

Having published his first book, Ranke went on to practise what he preached in a succession of large, multi-volume works. Following his move to the University of Berlin he made a series of research trips around Europe, exploring the archival material that he used for his books. For the first time historians relied primarily upon original sources rather than printed editions or compilations. He made particularly extensive use of the records left by Venetian ambassadors. However, what made Ranke and his pupils truly significant was not only the establishing of a methodology, but the institutional context in which this took place. This made their achievement permanent and greater and more effective than it would otherwise have been.

The key context was the reform of the university in Germany, beginning with the establishment of the University of Berlin by Wilhelm Von Humboldt (1767–1835) in 1810. The German university became in matters of curriculum, organization and structure the model for similar institutions all over the world, not least in the United States. By the eighteenth century European universities had fallen a long way from their medieval origins and had become almost the last place where one would look for scholarship or original thought. Gibbon's scathing view of Oxford was not unique. The 'new model' university created by Humboldt combined research with teaching and organized the university by the newly emerging academic disciplines as well as introducing new subjects to the curriculum.

Ranke established one of the central elements of modern historical research with his creation of a graduate seminar in history at Berlin in 1833. This made possible the systematic training of young historians and the passing on of knowledge and technique from one generation to another. The combination of research and teaching meant that there was a steady supply of graduates to enter the seminar and take up research. It also served the vital purpose of compelling the scholars to describe their work in an understandable form and so checked the constant tendency of academic research to wander off into the obscure and abstruse. Again, it created a community of scholars. While realized in Germany by the 1840s, it would be another generation before the same would be true of other countries such as England and France. There the tradition of the individual gentleman scholar persisted. As F. W. Maitland put it: 'We had our swallows, and beautiful birds they were; but there was spring in Germany.'[10]

Another important event was the founding in 1823 of the *Monumenta Germaniae Historica*. This was a great collective enterprise, founded by the Prussian statesman Stein, to bring out critical scholarly editions of all of the important sources for German medieval history and so make them readily available to historians. The first volume appeared in 1826, the second in 1829. Thereafter, they appeared in a steady stream (the process is still continuing, although rather more slowly) and today the number of volumes stands at over 360. This publishing programme made medieval German history possible for the first time. It also meant that each new historian no longer had to go through the arduous process of editing the source. Equally important was the foundation in 1859 of the *Historische Zeitschrift* by one of Ranke's pupils, Heinrich Von Sybel (1817–1895). This was the first professional historical journal with all of the features that are now familiar, such as reviews of publications, and articles based on original research and reviewed for publication in the journal by other scholars. The **'learned journal'** provided a forum for discussion and debate among scholars about the subjects of their research. It also provided a place where 'interim reports' could be made on continuing research and, as the years went by, came to embody the collective memory of the profession.

The last element in this set of institutions was the construction by the German universities of a structured career for scholars, passing from undergraduate study to full-fledged scholarship. The key element was the research-based further degree (PhD, DSc) which acted as a training or apprenticeship for the scholar and also enabled them to make a contribution to the process of academic research. What all of the institutions described did together was to make possible the modern phenomenon of a community of scholars, where thousands of people all over the world study a discipline with an agreed definition, using common research methods. This is of vital importance for an empirical subject such as history (or indeed the natural **sciences**) because it is this process of collective endeavour which makes possible the accumulation of knowledge, and checks the problems which inevitably arise in the pursuit of knowledge through empirical research.

Any individual researcher may, in all honesty, produce findings that are misleading or simply wrong, in whole or in part. This can happen in history because of sources that are corrupt or untypical, but the main problem is the inevitably partial viewpoint of the individual historian. This is not so much a matter of conscious bias as of the unconscious presuppositions which the individual scholar brings to the research, the limitations of the background knowledge available to them, and the way their perspective on past events is affected by their own specific historical location. If historians were isolated individuals and relatively few in number (as they were until the nineteenth century), this would have serious consequences. Its effects are now mitigated over time because each historian has to engage in a dialogue with many others and this checks the errors and misunderstandings or misplaced emphases of any one individual or group.

▶ The spread of professional history

Although modern scholarship began in Germany, it spread to other countries, although only after a delay of about a generation. In the United States the American Historical Association was founded in 1884, with its own learned journal, the *American Historical Review*. In Britain the **Regius** chairs in history at Oxford and Cambridge had been created by George I, but for many years the holders of these posts did little or no academic work. By the later nineteenth century things had improved, with J. R. Seeley (1834–1895) and William Stubbs (1829–1901) marking a turning point with their tenure of the chairs from 1869 to 1895 and 1866 to 1883, at Cambridge and Oxford respectively. Outside the universities the main events were the establishment of the Records Commission by Parliament in 1802. This was followed by the setting up in 1857 of a government financed series of editions of medieval sources, in conscious imitation of the *Monumenta*, usually known as the Rolls Series (because it had been set up by Sir Samuel Romilly, the Master of the Rolls). The Public Record Office for all government papers was set up in 1838 and finally opened in 1856. The Record Office immediately started the publication of the various series of **calendars** of State Papers. Meanwhile, learned societies such as the Surtees and Cheetham Societies began to publish records of relevance for provincial and local history. This process, starting in Germany but emulated all over Europe, made the practice of historical research immeasurably easier than before. The rise of professional scholarship was complete in most countries by the early twentieth century.[11]

▶ Critics of empirical history

The empirical approach described earlier and associated with Ranke was undoubtedly the predominant one among historians in both Europe and America by 1900. In some ways this revealed a misunderstanding of his ideas. Some understood the Rankean approach as meaning that the author should not have any presence in their work, but should have the role almost of an amanuensis, simply relaying the facts uncovered by research to the reader. Iggers has convincingly argued that this view was a misunderstanding of Ranke's ideas, which still left a crucial role of interpretation for the historian.[12] In any case, the new professional historians did not follow such an impossible creed in reality and many did not even claim to do so in theory. However, there were many who questioned the kind of empiricism advocated by historians such as Ranke and Mommsen and as the nineteenth century drew to its end, these criticisms and other ways of defining historical methodology became more prominent.

One frequent argument against empirical history derived from the belief that historical research or writing should serve a moral or political purpose. People who put this view typically argued that the claim to disinterested pursuit of the truth was simply impossible. From this perspective history was not an end in itself, but a way of serving some other, higher end: to pretend otherwise was at best naïve, at worst disingenuous. One such author was Acton who, although agreeing in most respects with empirical method, believed that historians had the task of subjecting the past to moral judgement because there were timeless moral standards by which the past could be judged.[13] A more common argument was that history had a public purpose and should serve a political end such as the strength of the state, the sustaining of national consciousness, or the belief in democratic and republican principles. As the above shows, this view was taken by people from all parts of the political spectrum of the time. In Germany this was the view of the so-called 'Prussian school' of Sybel, Droysen (1808–1884) and Treitschke (1834–1896) whose argument was for an engaged history that would promote both a German national identity and support for the unification of Germany by Prussia.[14] A similar but politically opposed view was taken by those who argued for a history that would serve the cause of liberty, such as Jules Michelet (1798–1874) or E. A. Freeman (1823–1892). A more general form of the argument was that historians inevitably had predispositions and prejudices and should be judged on how far they could support these by using the sources at their disposal, so making history a form of **advocacy**. This was effectively the position of J. A. Froude, which is reflected in the passage quoted earlier in the Introduction (p. 7).

A related but distinct set of beliefs that challenged straightforward empiricism were the ideas of what is usually called 'historical **romanticism**'. This is usually associated with French thought, and particularly the work of Michelet, Augustin Thierry (1795–1856) and Edgar Quinet (1803–1875), but its main ideas were found in other countries as well.[15] The romantic approach, in history as much as art and literature, was both a development of, and reaction against, the classicism, universalism and rationalism of the Enlightenment. The emphasis is on sentiment and feeling as opposed to rational calculation, the particular and local as against the universal, and (frequently) the medieval in contrast to both ancient and modern. In historiography this set of attitudes was worked out in a number of ways. It meant support for an approach that was passionate and committed rather than detached. It led to a focus upon communities of shared consciousness or sentiment, most notably the nation, as the subjects of historical inquiry. However, the focus was not primarily upon the leaders or rulers but on the total community. Hence, there was an attempt to examine the total experience of a past community, all aspects of their life, in order to understand it fully, and in particular to recapture their subjective experience or consciousness. In its view of the historian's role, romanticism led to an emphasis on the necessary and desirable place of feeling and emotion in the process of historical research. It also meant an emphasis upon literary skill, and writing that was intended to inspire emotion as well as to convey information. This all challenged the empirical approach, with its emphasis on the search for source-based knowledge and interpretation rather than sentiment.

▶ The positivist challenge

The ideas just described could be combined with an empirical approach, although in practice this did not happen. The more fundamental challenge to empiricism came from two other approaches, which questioned the whole basis of empirical historical reasoning as it had developed by the nineteenth century. One was **positivism**, the other philosophical **idealism**. It may seem strange to bracket these two intellectual movements together, as positivism is usually seen as allied to an empirical theory of knowledge, while idealism is the main rival to empiricism in

epistemology. However, several ways of thinking about history which have been very influential combine both of them. They also share a fundamental common premiss, that there is an underlying structure or order to the world, including the human world and human history, which historians can uncover, and to do so is essential to full understanding on the historian's part.

Positivism is a much-used and much-debated term. It can refer to a specific nineteenth-century intellectual and philosophical movement. It also has a more general meaning in the philosophy of knowledge. In this latter sense it means the belief that, first, the methods of the natural sciences are the only reliable source of knowledge and, second, that those methods involve the accumulation of empirical facts from which universally applicable patterns will emerge. Positivism in this sense is a specific kind of empiricism, one which combines the empirical theory of knowledge with a specific argument about the form which that knowledge will take and the method to be used to attain it.[16]

Applying positivism to history leads to the belief that history could and should be a science like the natural sciences such as physics. In other words, it means that there can be a science of human action and human society, whether in the present or the past, which has the same quality and explanatory power as a natural science. According to this way of thinking, the study of the material world (including the human world) yields statistically significant patterns which are the basis for general laws. These have both an explanatory and a predictive aspect, that is, they both explain why particular events occur and predict how and when they will happen in the future. So the goal of a positivist history is to identify and determine general historical laws which will be true for all times and places, will explain the observable patterns found in the past, and will also, by extrapolation, predict the future. Sophisticated positivism allows that it will not be possible to predict or explain the actions of individuals, but argues that statistical regularities make it possible to make definite statements about human actions in the aggregate. Examples of such historical 'laws' that have been put forward by various authors include 'complex societies always arise in temperate climates rather than tropical ones', 'the history of societies is the history of class conflict', and 'the mixture of races is fatal to civilization'.

Positivist methodology enjoyed great respect in the nineteenth and early twentieth centuries because it was seen (incorrectly) as the methodology of natural science, which enjoyed great intellectual prestige. One of the earliest thinkers to advocate the application of these ideas to the study of human society, including its history, was the Frenchman Henri Saint-Simon (1760–1825). Although not a historian himself he founded a school of writers who were, and it was through them that positivism first entered historical argument. The key figure in the development of this argument was his intellectual heir Auguste Comte (1798–1857). It was Comte who took the ideas of positivism and created an actual intellectual movement, Positivism. In his major work *Course of Positive Philosophy* (1830–42) he set out an elaborate schema for a scientific model of history. This divided human history into three stages, each of which corresponded to a phase in the development of the human mind. These were the theological-military (the ancient world), the metaphysical-legalistic (the medieval world), and the scientific-industrial (the modern world). Apart from noting that Comte, like all prophets, saw his own time as the culmination of human experience, two observations are worth making. The first is that positivism, while almost entirely forgotten today, had a great influence on nineteenth-century thinking, in Britain as much as his native France. The other is that Comtean positivism derived much of its appeal from the felt need for an alternative to, or replacement for, the old idea of divine providence. The Rankean rejection of teleology in history and its emphasis on the particular rather than the general were felt to be unsatisfying, removing the element of purpose and transcendental meaning from history, which the doctrine of providence had supplied. Positivism was one of several systems of thought that sought to fill this gap.

As well as Comte, there were several other thinkers who tried to develop a positivist model of history, that is, one which would generate universal laws of historical development and causation. One, a great success in his time but almost forgotten now, was Henry Thomas Buckle (1821–1862). An autodidact, Buckle became famous for his *History of Civilisation in England* (1857–1861). In this he sought to develop a science of man which could explain the history of civilization by reference to such matters as climate, geography and innate psychology. Another pioneering sociologist who incorporated laws of history into his analysis and had great influence in his day was Herbert Spencer (1820–1903). He argued for a theory of history centred on the distinction between 'military' societies and 'industrial' ones. To his distress the anticipated course of history went into reverse during his own lifetime.

Among historians who adopted positivism the most forceful advocate of the 'history as science' approach was the French scholar Numa-Denis Fustel de Coulanges (1830–89). Fustel's positivism was an extreme form of empiricism, which denied the existence (as opposed to the knowability) of what could not be perceived. His argument was that if history adopted this position, it could make positive statements about the past which would have as great an authority as the propositions of science. A similar view was taken by the Anglo-Irish historian J. B. Bury (1861–1927), most notably in his inaugural lecture as Regius professor at Cambridge. (In later life Bury moved away from this and came to argue for the essential role played by chance and fortuitous circumstances in historical causation: such things are by their nature unpredictable, irregular and not susceptible to scientific analysis.)[17]

However, the best known of those writers who tried to create a **positivist science** of history was Karl Marx (not forgetting the important part played by

Engels). The Marxist schema of history is another attempt to found explanations on a number of general principles that apply to all human societies and, like most such schemes, generates a picture of history as a process, leading through stages to a final goal. It is with Marx that we can see most clearly the connection between the positivist idea of history as a science with its own laws, and the other main challenge to orthodox empiricism, philosophical idealism.

▶ The idealist alternative

Idealism, like empiricism, is a theory of knowledge. Like empiricism, it can be traced back to the ancient Greeks, particularly Plato. Again like empiricism, the fully worked forms of idealist epistemology are complex, but the underlying principle is simple. It is that knowledge of the world depends not on experience, but on ideas or the structure of the mind that observes it. In the modern world the most important philosophers in this tradition are Kant and Hegel. History has a central part in Hegel's version of idealism. For Hegel the underlying reality, which is timeless and eternal, is not the physical world but '*Geist*', usually translated as 'spirit'. Through time (that is, in the course of history) the perceived world comes ever closer to the underlying real world. This is achieved by the mechanism of the **dialectic**. In every age there is the dominant idea or perception of reality, the 'thesis', which is confronted by its contradictory idea, the 'antithesis'. Eventually, these are combined and reconciled in a higher level and more complete idea, the 'synthesis'. Applied to human history, this means that history must be understood as the unfolding or realization of an underlying reality.[18] Marx combined this philosophical model with a positivist search for the general laws that would explain the unfolding and its progress. He found this in the development not of ideas, but of the 'material productive forces', that is, the ways that human beings transform the physical world to meet their needs. This was called '**dialectical materialism**', because it combined the dialectical process with a **materialist** explanation for change.

There are many philosophers of history who have been influenced by Hegel and other idealist philosophers, but they do not try, as Marx did, to combine the Hegelian view of history as the realization of an idea, with a materialist explanation of historical change. It is revealing that the best known proponents of idealist theories of history are all primarily philosophers, rather than practising historians, even if they do history 'on the side'. Examples of this are the Italian Benedetto Croce (1866–1952), and the Englishman R. G. Collingwood (1889–1943).[19] Most historians have remained empiricist in practice, even if they have paid attention to the criticisms of the idealists. Criticisms there certainly have been, for, from the late nineteenth century onwards, this has been the principal source of fundamental critique of empirical historical reasoning. Initially, such attacks focus on the extreme position of the positivist historians such as Fustel, but the Rankean mainstream of empirical history increasingly comes in for critical comment. The most important figure in this process was the German philosopher Wilhelm Dilthey (1833–1911).

▶ Dilthey and ultra-historicism

Dilthey's work is both an attack on empirical history and also an attempt to incorporate its insights into an idealist account of the human world. His starting point was Kantian epistemology. Kant had argued that our knowledge of the world is derived not from sense impressions, but from the inherent structures or categories of the human mind, such as temporality (the perception of time as moving in one direction and being divided into past, present and future). For Kant these structures were ahistorical, that is, they were the same for all human beings in all times. Dilthey accepted Kant's basic thesis but argued that the structures of the human mind were not universal but historically specific, that is, the product of particular times and circumstances. This means that the way the world is perceived by one observer at one time is different from the perception of it by another observer at another time. Dilthey's thought was thus radically historicist. It has far-reaching implications for history as a discipline. If all individuals, including historians, have an understanding of the world (including the past) which is determined by their own situation, then there can be no way of simply recounting 'what actually occurred'. Two historians from different epochs will perceive the same events in different ways and there is no timeless perspective from which one can judge between their accounts. It also becomes impossible to have a transgenerational project of historical research, in which successive generations of historians build on each other's research to move towards a greater degree of certainty about the past.

Dilthey made a further criticism of positivist approaches by arguing that there were two distinct kinds of systematic study of the world, the natural sciences and the human sciences. The methods of one were not appropriate to the other. He argued that the key to knowledge in the human sciences was that the practitioner could realistically attempt to achieve an empathic understanding (**Verstehen**) of their subject (human beings and their interactions) which was not possible in the case of inanimate objects. The main way of achieving this was **hermeneutics**. Originally, this meant the systematic study of legal or biblical texts so as to extract their possible meanings, but for Dilthey it was a method for understanding the totality of human experience, interpreted as a system of (historically located) signs and signals.[20] These ideas reappear in critiques of empiricism up to today. Collingwood, for example, argued that historical understanding was possible if the historically shaped historian could re-enact the events he was studying in his mind so as to achieve the subjective understanding he needed.

By the later nineteenth century, then, empirical history had been defined both as a worked out theory of historical method and as a practice on the part of professional historians. This had also provoked a number of reactions. One, that of positivism, argued in effect that the moderate empiricism of the Rankeans was too modest and too much attached to the particular rather than the general. For these authors the goal of empirical research was to achieve a scientific level of knowledge and certainty, and in particular to uncover the laws of history. Others attacked the underlying philosophical basis of the discipline. However, although influential, neither of these currents of thought ultimately had much effect on the way historians worked and wrote, even if they paid them lip service.

▶ The persistence of empirical method

Positivism in both senses of the word had a considerable appeal for a while but fell foul of two factors; the persistence of nominalism among historians and the brutal realities of historical evidence. For a science of history to work, 'forces' or 'entities' which lay behind the laws of history (such as 'class conflict' and 'race') had to be as real and universal as, say, gravity or magnetism. Historians proved very reluctant to give real existence to such categories of analysis. More important was the nature of historical evidence. Even if the existence of general laws of historical causation are admitted, it becomes very difficult to discern them in the plethora of detail thrown up by research. In fact, most historians do not admit the existence of such laws, arguing that the evidence simply does not support claims for predictive regularity in historical causation. For every generalization there are too many, often major, exceptions. This does not mean that generalizations are useless, but does mean that they cannot be held to have the universal quality of a scientific law. In addition, historians like Bury came to argue that features of the human world, such as free will, and the crucial role of individuals and random chance in historical causation, made attempts to apply the techniques of natural science to history theoretically, as well as practically, impossible.

The challenge of idealism had both less and more impact. Less in some senses because most historians were baffled by the philosophy, which ran counter to the basic assumptions of their discipline as they had been taught it, and because it was seen as threatening to the career structure and organization of the profession. So the fundamental arguments of authors like Dilthey and Croce were not addressed. In other ways the impact was considerable. While not accepting the fundamental implications of Dilthey or Collingwood's historicism, historians such as Carl Becker (1873–1945) did accept the idea of the historian as a historically located figure, influenced and shaped by their context, and did come to argue for a more complex idea of what constituted a historical fact, allowing more scope for authorial subjectivity. However, historians did not generally accept that this made empirical history impossible, only that it made it difficult.

By about 1910 it had become clear what the workings of empirical history led to in practice. One often regretted result was that it led to the appearance of a scholarly discussion, in the pages of monographs and journals, which was increasingly separate from the wider public debate. Another was the early appearance of the dialectic of historical debate, the main spur to the growth of historical knowledge. In this process initial research into a historical topic will lead to a broadly agreed view or orthodoxy. This is then challenged by a new generation of younger historians (inevitably known as 'revisionists'). In time they triumph and establish a new orthodoxy. This is then challenged in its turn by a new generation of 'young turks', who often start off by reassessing the discarded orthodoxy of the first generation. Outsiders (and philosophers in particular) often present this process as simply a matter of fad and fashion, with ideas simply being recycled like old styles of dress in the clothing industry. Alternatively it is seen as a product of contemporary politics, which leads young historians to ask particular questions of the past. These views imply that historiographical debates do not lead to any growth of knowledge.

In fact, this is not true. As we shall see, it is not the case that old orthodoxy is discarded *tout court* like last year's style. Rather, elements of the old are incorporated into the new and with time, certain hypotheses are either moved into the category of the 'almost certain' or are discarded for good as 'certainly false'. The result is a slow, crabwise, but definite growth of knowledge. In other words, the number of statements that can be made about a historical topic increases and the degree of certainty that can be attached to an increasing number of them becomes greater. Complete certainty and agreement is never reached, but certain debates are, after a while, generally agreed to be 'closed'. Just as in mathematics an infinite series can have a finite sum, so historical debate moves towards a conclusion without ever actually arriving. The degree to which it approaches that state is determined by a number of factors, the most important being the nature and extent of the surviving evidence.

One apparent result of this is that historians' arguments come to focus on ever-smaller issues, so they argue more and more about less and less. This is corrected (thank heavens!) by the third major aspect of the progress of empirical history, its extension into ever-wider areas of human experience. Initially, empirical history was concerned mainly with the history of certain periods and topics, particularly political history and the history of institutions such as law and government. The early twentieth century saw the appearance of the so-called 'new history'. This phenomenon has repeated itself several times. It involves the study by historians of new topics of historical inquiry or classes of source material or the adoption of new methods for investigating them. This is sometimes presented as a move away from empirical history, because empirical methods are seen as necessarily implying that politics and institutions are the only respectable areas of study for the historian. Certainly, some well-known empiricist historians have taken this view. However, on closer examination it turns out that in most cases these new departures are actually the application of empirical methods to new areas, and they reveal its extension rather than its demise.

3 The Transformation of Biography in Empirical History

▶ The relationship between history and biography

The connection between history and biography would seem to be a close and natural one. Most biographies, after all, are accounts of the lives of dead men and women and so fall within the domain of the historian, that is, the study of the human past. Conversely, if history is in fact the study of past human experience, what could be more germane than the accounts of the actual lives and actions of specific human beings? Moreover, in many times and places, such as medieval Europe, much of what was written about the past was built around accounts of the lives of prominent figures, be they rulers, clerics or saints. Biography was, then, the core or heart of **historiography**.

This can be clearly seen in the works of many medieval writers. Froissart's *Chronicles* were written to preserve the memory of the lives and deeds of his contemporaries. The twelfth-century chronicler Otto of Freising wrote an account of his own times through a life of the Emperor Frederic Barbarossa. Even works with a thematic approach, such as Bede's *Ecclesiastical History*, were organized around the accounts of the lives of individuals who had played a prominent part in the story Bede wished to tell, such as Aidan, Cuthbert and Northumbrian rulers such as Edwin and Oswald.

However, despite this close connection many distinguished historians have argued that biography is not properly part of the historian's remit and should be consigned to the sphere of literature. This is one of the few points of agreement between Carr and Elton, although their reasons for slighting the importance of biography were revealingly different. For Carr, looking at the lives of individual men and women exaggerated the role of individuals and their actions in historical causation and underemphasized the part played by impersonal structures and human beings in the mass.[1] Elton, while more receptive to arguments which gave a place to the lives and choices of individuals, felt that these had to take second place to the study of institutions and that biography as a method ran the risk of importing literary ideas and techniques into the study of history, where they were not appropriate.

On the other hand, biography, both individual and collective, has been and continues to be a major element of historiography. Norman Gash, himself the author of a distinguished biography (of Sir Robert Peel), is one historian who has defended the practice of biography as both methodologically defensible and useful. He argues that through a study of the life of an individual, we can learn things and acquire a perspective which would not be available without this form of study. Derek Beales is another self-conscious defender of the biographer's art.[2]

This controversy arises because biography does raise issues for historians. In the first place it raises the question of individual agency in history, of the significance of individuals and their actions and personal qualities for historical explanation. Arguably, biography, or the biographical approach to history, leads to an emphasis on the consequences of the choices and actions of individuals. So, for example, a life of Charles Stuart Parnell will inevitably emphasize the consequences of Parnell's character and his relationship with Kitty O'Shea for the wider course of Anglo–Irish relations and Irish Nationalist politics. This is troublesome for historians such as Carr who argue for a **structuralist** view of human action, in which the range of choices open to individuals is constrained and the consequences of those choices, even when made by people with power or influence, are relatively unimportant. A history of Irish Nationalism written from this point of view would emphasize the way social and economic structures limited the room for manoeuvre of politicians such as Parnell or Gladstone, and would see Parnell's personal problems as having no long-term significance. The explanatory weight would instead rest upon structural economic and political change, in which even prominent individuals played only a minor part. It is hard to imagine writing a life of a historical character on this basis, certainly, if one did, it would lead to a book that was both pointless and dull.

The counter-argument of course is that the role of individuals *is* important, that historical events are not determined by impersonal forces and that, consequently, individuals matter. The extreme view is that of Thomas Carlyle, in which history consists of the deeds of great men. As he put it: 'For, as I take it, Universal History, the history of what man has accomplished in this world, is at the bottom the history of the great men who have worked here.'[3] In this view all history is in some sense subsumed within biography: its function is to provide a backdrop or stage set for the biographer's narrative. No historian would now take Carlyle's view. Empirical historians, however, do tend to emphasize the importance of individual agency in historical explanation, even though they also recognize that all historical actors are constrained to some degree. This is because their **scepticism** about structural explanations in general leaves room for explanations that depend on the part played by chance or the decisions made by individuals.

A different objection is the one made by Elton, since it derives from that view of the historian's purpose that, as we saw, is intimately associated with the empirical approach to history. The fear is that the demands of the literary form of the biography will shape and determine the kind of work that is produced. Thus, the historian who writes a biography and makes a person's life their subject matter will be led, almost against their will, to structure their account around literary rather than historical concerns. There will be a tendency to construct a discernible plot with a beginning, middle and end, even where this might not be appropriate or in accordance with the evidence. There is a temptation to make the life story conform to one of the two genres of tragedy and comedy.

A significant fear is that literary concerns will lead to unwarranted speculation, especially regarding such matters as the feelings and emotions of the subject, for which there may be no empirical evidence. The most serious concern however is the reality that most biographies have been written for a present-minded purpose, for some reason other than the search, however difficult, for the truth. This contradicts the principle that the historian should seek to understand the past on its own terms. There is a strong suspicion that biography is particularly prone to this 'present-minded' approach.

As a form of historiography, biography certainly does have some distinctive features. There is a focus on the character and psychology of the subject as much as the events in which they were involved. As Jordanova observes, biographies have a natural **chronology**, which comes from taking the span of an individual human life as a unit of time.[4] There *is* an emphasis on human agency, even in those cases where the subject is chosen as a kind of 'everyman' figure, to exemplify the lives of others indistinguishable from the subject except for the lack of records. For the more empirically minded historian, the purpose of a biography is to give an account of the events and course of the subject's life, to relate that and (in the case of prominent or public figures) to describe the part played in the events of that time by the subject. However, this can be done only by reference to the **sources** and must be conducted in the same way as all empirical research, that is, as far as possible, without a present-minded motive.

▶ Classical and medieval biography

This is, however, a very modern way of thinking. Until very recently it would have struck most writers of biography as absurd and morally reprehensible. Biography is one of the oldest forms of writing. One of the most famous biographers, and the model for many of those who followed him, was the first/second-century author Plutarch. Revealingly, Plutarch was primarily a moral philosopher rather than a historian. Despite having written in this area (the *Moralia*), he is best known for a series of biographies, usually known as the *Parallel Lives.* These give accounts, 46 in all, of the lives of famous Greeks and Romans, arranged in 23 contrasting pairs, each of one Greek and one Roman. Clearly, these are in some senses works of history. However, this was not Plutarch's main concern when he wrote them. His purpose was to use the lives to explore questions of character, virtue and fortune, and the part these played in the lives of famous individuals. He also wanted to draw comparisons and contrasts between the two cultures of Greece and Rome (hence the pairings). In other words, the lives were written not for their own sake, but for an external purpose, a mixture of education and analysis.

In this as in other respects, Plutarch was a model for the writers who came after him. The late ancient and medieval period saw the production of many biographies and, as mentioned earlier, many works which were not explicitly biographical were still organized around the lives of principal figures from the period or geographical area they were looking at. The biographies written in this period were, like Plutarch's *Lives*, written for reasons external to the subject matter itself. We can classify these goals of biography under four principal headings, those of entertainment, memory, admonition and example. Each of these tended to produce its own kind of narrative structure and, when combined with particular subject matter, led to the appearance of distinct sub-genres of biography. All of these purposes still persist in much contemporary biographical writing, as do the sub-genres they produce.

The goal of entertainment is a simple and obvious one. Here the aim of the biographer is to evoke emotion or feeling in the reader, to amuse or give rise to sentiments such as admiration, pity and affection. Biography of this sort is very close to avowed fiction, with the difference that the principal character is a person who has actually existed rather than a fictional one drawn from the mind of the writer. Biographies with this as their primary goal are a staple of popular culture, from the Middle Ages down to the present day.

A more serious purpose for biography, which lay behind many of those produced in the medieval period, is that of memory. Here the life of a person is recounted so that the memory of their life and deeds will not be lost with the passage of time. The purpose therefore is to freeze or preserve the memories of those now alive in the form of a text, which will transmit them through time to subsequent generations. The focus is often upon the acts or deeds of the person, hence the frequent use during the medieval period of the term '*gesta*' (that is 'deeds') as the title of such works. The crucial concept that grows out of this concern with deeds and the remembrance of them is that of 'fame', meaning reputation or renown, particularly of the posthumous variety. It was the work of a biographer that transformed the temporary memory of those who had observed the acts of the person into the more permanent phenomenon of fame. The importance of this as a motive for biography (and indeed for historiography more generally) can be seen from passages such as this well known one from Froissart:

> In order that the honourable enterprises, noble adventures and deeds of arms which took place during the wars waged by France and England should be fittingly related and preserved for posterity, so that the brave should be inspired thereby to follow such examples. I wish to place on record these matters of renown.[5]

One consequence of the concern for fame was that those who sought it were concerned for their reputation not only in the eyes of their contemporaries, but also in posterity.

The passage from Froissart also highlights what was perhaps the most frequent motive for biography, that of example. The idea was that the account of the life would provide a model or example for readers to emulate. The reverse of this was the admonitory biography, which told a tale as a means of emphasizing human failings and so giving an example of conduct to avoid. Sometimes the two were combined, as in many saints' lives, with an admonitory first part of the life followed by an exemplary later section. This all made biography a form of moral instruction rather than historiography. In literary terms they could be located in the genres of comedy, tragedy or romance. One consequence was that in biography, as in other forms of medieval historiography, the form was as important as the content.

There were many outstanding medieval biographies. Examples include the *Life of Charlemagne* by Einhard, the *Gesta Frederici* of Otto of Freising, and the *Life of Saint Louis* by Joinville. However, they reveal the gap between such works and modern, empirically based historical biography. Because the primary purpose of the authors was edification or instruction, the evidence of events was included or omitted to fit the purpose. Joinville, for example, includes accounts of miraculous 'events' because these assist his intention of telling the exemplary life of a man who combined the roles of king and saint. Einhard presents a picture designed to elevate Charlemagne and his dynasty at the expense of the Merovingians. Even more dramatic was the way that literary traditions and forms were allowed to dictate content. Einhard, for example, based his *Life* very closely on the model of Suetonius's *Lives of the Caesars* and forced the events of his own time to conform to the plot and structure of that work. Otto of Freising also let much of his work be shaped in this way. So, for example, the description of the physical appearance of Frederic in his work is taken verbatim from Einhard's *Life of Charlemagne* and from the account of Theodoric the Ostrogoth by the Gothic chronicler Jordanes. In general, medieval biography was a form of narrative based upon, or making use of, real events, but using this to create a work designed for purposes such as edification and incorporating supposition and outright invention in the process – all very **postmodern** in fact!

There were, as said, sub-genres of biography produced by the combinations of purpose and subject matter. The most popular in terms of the number produced (although maybe not read?) were lives of saints or **hagiography**. The other main type was lives of rulers or members of the aristocracy. These had a considerable overlap in content with the purely fictional narrative of romance and chivalry. Towards the end of the medieval period other kids of subject matter appeared. The most notable were lives of artists and this produced one of the first examples of collective biography in the *Lives of the Artists* by Vasari, first published in 1550.

From the sixteenth century onwards a new, related form made its appearance in the shape of the autobiography. However, it is fair to say that as late as 1850 biography remained primarily a literary form and had been little affected by the growth of empirical historical technique. In fact, it is notable just how persistent the traditional ideas of the purpose of biography actually were. The idea of the exemplary life was as strong as ever and found expression in a whole catalogue of lives of worthy figures. One good example of this is the many biographical works produced by Samuel Smiles. The kinds of people chosen for celebration were certainly new: Smiles chose to write about engineers rather than kings or bishops, but the essential form and purpose was unchanged.

▶ Empirical biography in the nineteenth century

From about the mid-nineteenth century onwards attempts *were* made to produce biographies that could conform to the newly established principles of historical scholarship. These initially took the form of the massive, multi-volume 'official' lives that weigh down the shelves of second-hand bookshops. The standard nineteenth-century biographies were in many ways an advance on what had gone before. There was some attempt at neutrality, at writing the life from a detached viewpoint rather than producing an apologia. There was a growing convention that the life should be based, as far as possible, on the public record and private papers produced by the subject. This frequently took the form of incorporating primary texts such as speeches and, above all, correspondence into the narrative. Some authors effectively incorporated the entire private papers of their subject into their work. This is one reason for the enormous bulk of so many of them.

There was a definite movement, as the century went on, in the direction of what became known as the 'life and times' model of biography. In this, while the narrative of the individual life provided the structure of the work, this was located in a more wide ranging historical account of the period in which the subject had lived. This provided a context for the life and made the nature and actions of the subject more comprehensible. It also made it possible to describe and assess the impact of the person's own life and deeds on the events of their time and the lives of others. This was a major advance, since it gave the biography a concrete historicity, by locating it in a wider historical narrative. It also made possible nuanced judgements about the role and impact of the individual subject in the cause of historical events, avoiding both structural determinism and Carlyle's 'Great Man' theory.

Nevertheless, nineteenth-century and early twentieth-century biography still had severe limitations. Many works still showed a strong tendency towards hagiography and the exemplary. Even works that avoided this generally followed the maxim 'speak no ill of the dead' and embarrassing or compromising aspects of the subject's life were ignored and passed over in a discreet silence. (The same was true until recently of obituaries which developed a set of coded expressions such as 'confirmed bachelor' to convey details that could not be explicitly spelt out). This was mercilessly satirized and attacked by Lytton Strachey in *Eminent Victorians* and in some ways the genre of the exemplary life has never recovered.[6]

The reliance upon documentary evidence and the avoiding of pure invention was an undoubted breakthrough. Indeed, the incorporation of large quantities of **primary** material into the text makes many of these works a useful introduction to the sources for present-day historians. However, the documents were presented raw and undigested, they were not analysed and little actual use was made of them. Instead, they were presented simply to illustrate or to convey a point without any interruption of analysis by the author.

The best biographies of this kind are still worth reading, both as literature and as introductions to the topic. (In some cases they are essential reading because no one has written or undertaken a satisfactory replacement.) Among the best are G. M. Trevelyan's lives of John Bright and Guiseppe Garibaldi, Sandburg's life of Abraham Lincoln, and the lives of Richard Cobden and W. E. Gladstone by John Morley. One biographical work from the nineteenth century which was both an important work of scholarship and a vital resource for future generations of historians was the *Dictionary of National Biography*, the brainchild of George Smith, an entrepreneurial publisher, and its editor Leslie Stephen. This produced 29,120 lives over 15 years. In doing so it provided both an important biographical resource and established standards for what we may term the 'minimal' biography, based purely on personal knowledge and empirical evidence.[7]

▶ The nature and qualities of empirical biography

It was the demands of such works that defined the qualities of empirical biography, that is, lives that employed a strictly empirical methodology. Clearly, the starting point is that biography of this kind can be based only upon information gained from the sources, whether direct or indirect. This means that much of the traditional content will frequently be dismissed as **mythical** or speculative. Such matters as the psychological state of the subject cannot be addressed unless there is some empirical warrant for it in the shape of such sources as letters, diaries or an autobiography, and even then only with great caution. Acts or events for which no evidence can be found in written records will be handled very sceptically, if indeed they are admitted at all. There will be no place for the kind of complete invention found in some biographies, where events or speeches are interpolated to assist the plot or because they seem feasible.

The sources needed for producing an empirical biography are of a distinctive kind. A figure who has played a major part in public life such as a monarch or leading politician or soldier may have ample evidence of their life in so far as there are records extant of events in which they were involved. From such evidence it is possible to construct an account of the public life of that person. However, this would be a life lacking in most kinds of human detail, one in which the office comes close to swallowing up the man or woman. The records needed for a full biography are of a more personal nature. The most immediately personal are such things as diaries and commonplace books. A diary that is simply a journal, that is, a record of events on a day-to-day basis, is still very useful, not least for settling matters of precise **chronology**. One which contains reflections on events or is confessional can give real insight into the psychology and state of mind of the author. Most people, however, either do not keep a diary or do so only for particular periods of their life. An autobiography can also be valuable in the same way, not least for what it tells us *against* the intent of the author. It may also contain information that would otherwise be unavailable. The most common kind of personal record though is correspondence, and letters and private papers are the basis of almost all important biographies. These can provide information about most of the things that the biographer wants to know, including the subject's state of mind, their relations with other people, their personality, and the details of their actions.

However, these sources are often difficult to use and interpret. The problem for some historians is their subjective quality, as opposed to the supposedly more objective public records. This means that the historian who uses records such as private correspondence has to be constantly aware of the viewpoint of the author and its limitations. However, this is actually the case for most primary sources and in the case of biography the viewpoint and perspective of the subject is precisely what the historian wishes to capture or uncover.

The more serious difficulty arises with respect to the *nature* of records such as diaries and letters. The common presumption is that such texts are private rather than public, that is, they are written to be read only by the person to whom they are addressed or even (in the case of a diary) only by the writer. This gives them a more immediate, direct quality: we get an insight into the writers thinking, which is not concealed by the need to observe niceties or think of the impact of one's words on public opinion. The problem is that this is not always true. Diaries can be written with an eye to future publication, even if only posthumously. The same is true of letters, particularly those written by public figures, who may well write either with an eye to posterity or in the expectation that a supposedly private communication may be made public. Autobiographies are commonly written for purposes of self-justification. In fact, their greatest use for the historian frequently is to provide a guide to the author's view of themselves rather than the facts of their life. All this means that personal records have to be used with great caution.

In many cases though, they do not exist at all or only in trivial quantities. In such cases the historian has to rely on the kind of public records mentioned earlier and accounts of the subject written by contemporaries. There are also sometimes records when the subject has been in contact in some way with an institution which has left records. This can have surprising or ironic results. For example the records of the Inquisition contain a great deal of biographical detail about the unlucky persons brought before their tribunals. The result is that for people from Catholic countries who were not members of the elite, extensive information is most likely to survive if they were in trouble with the Holy Office for heresy or some other offence. For many people in the past, the only way they were likely to generate any detailed record was if they came into contact with a bureaucratic agency of the state.

An empirical biography is one strictly based upon the available evidence. It is not written to hold up a model life for emulation by future generations, nor is it intended to serve a purpose in contemporary politics and argument. However, the account of the subject's life is not simply a self-contained end in itself, as if the subject were an asocial isolate. The aim is to reconstruct as much as can be known of the events and course of the subject's life and to locate or place it in the wider historical narrative, and in so doing explain and describe the significance of that life for the wider narrative. Where the life in question is that of a major figure the **narrative** of that life enables us to better understand their acts and relations with other people and the part these played in determining the wider course of events. When it deals with a typical or illustrative individual, the value comes from the way one life can be made to stand for many others. Historical biography is a kind of archaeology of mind and character in which remnants or traces left by an individual in their passage through time and interaction with others in the course of that passage are examined and put together to construct a historically situated and contextualized life of that person.

This can be thought of as having four possible levels. The lowest level or skeleton is the basic chronological narrative of such events as birth, parentage, marriage (if any) and death. This is the kind of basic, skeletal, life that would be written for an entry in a work such as the *Dictionary of National Biography*. The second level is the detail of the person's actions and activities and their interactions with people close to them in one sense or another. The third is their relation to the wider historical society and period in which they lived. The final level is the account of the 'interior' person, their thoughts and feelings or rather (since this is all we can know) what they reveal of this in the record, whether deliberately or inadvertently. Several things follow from this.

First, the need to base the life account on empirical evidence means that it will not always be possible to construct a complete account which works on all four levels. For many historical figures, including some of real importance, we can do little more than the first level. An account which incorporates the fourth level is only really feasible if we have the kind of personal records described earlier. This is not the case for many important figures, including many in the twentieth century.

In such cases the biographer can only give an account of the events of the subject's public and private life. Their psychology is a matter only for speculation or (more properly) inference from their recorded actions and behaviour. In any account the relative importance given to levels two and three will depend on the nature of the subject and their life.

Second, applying strict criteria of evidence and analysis means that what we really know about even famous people in the past often proves to be much less that we often imagine. I myself vividly remember one of my undergraduate tutors telling several of us that all we could say for certain about King Alfred was the dates of his birth and death and a few events in his life. He exaggerated for effect, but not by much. The same point could be made of rulers and leading figures from many times and places, not only the European 'Dark Ages'.

Indeed in some cases the person dissolves once exposed to the harsh solvent of historical scholarship, until all of the details of their life and even their actual existence are called into question. A good example of this is the effect of repeated attempts to write a life of Jesus. The application of critical historical scholarship to the evidence of the New Testament and other sources such as Josephus has removed most of the detail found in traditional accounts. Some authors have come to the conclusion that the person of Jesus has no historicity, that is, that no such person ever actually existed. Instead, they argue that the figure of Jesus found in the Gospels is a composite fiction derived from a range of Jewish and other sources.

This kind of argument has also been made recently about a figure whose historicity is usually regarded as much more solid, the Prophet Muhammad. The traditional account of his life, as found in Islamic scholarship and the modern work of W. Montgomery Watt, has a wealth of detail, as well as a clear structure of dates for his birth, death and the significant events in his life. However, by using textual analysis of the Koran and other Islamic sources, John Wansbrough was able to undermine much of this narrative. His pupils Michael Cook and Patricia Crone have gone further, pointing out that the evidence we have for the life of Muhammad comes from almost 200 years after the events and is deeply unreliable on a number of counts. They conclude that we know very little for certain about him.[8]

This shows a third consequence of the empirical approach to biography, that it tends to dissolve and discredit myths attached to historical figures. This is not the same thing as the 'debunking' life, which often seeks to replace myths or ill-founded stories which show the subject in a positive light by ones which are scandalous but no better founded. An example of the destructive effect of scholarship upon myth can be seen through the examples given by Pieter Geyl in his *Napoleon: For and Against*.[9] It is clear from Geyl's account that the heroic myth of Napoleon was created principally by literary authors, while the historians produced a more critical but more accurate view. Another example is the case of Abraham Lincoln. Many of the earlier lives, culminating in Sandburg's massive work, presented his life in heroic terms while others, writing from a neo-confederate position, portray him in dark colours. The scholarly work of authors such as David Donald has arrived at a position which, while critical in many respects, does not accept either the positive or negative mythology of Lincoln as man and politician.[10]

The fourth consequence is one alluded to earlier, that regardless of the availability of sources, it is still more important to study the lives of outstanding individuals than those of average persons. A fundamental assumption in the writing of a meaningful biography is that the choices and actions of individuals are at least a factor in historical causation. To the extent that this is true, the lives of individuals who are prominent in some way (in politics, war, the arts or ideas, for example) will have effects far beyond their immediate circle of relatives and contacts. Putting together a historically located life of a significant individual enables us to understand the period better, inasmuch as we gain a better understanding of the part they played in shaping events. When dealing with the life of an ordinary person (including average members of the elite), the explanatory power and scope of the life account is much less. In such a case, the significance of the life for the historian lies in its typicality, the extent to which it is representative of the experience of a large class. What is common and shared becomes more important than what is unique and distinctive.

▶ Prosopography and psychohistory

It is this which lies behind the development in the twentieth century of a specialized form of biography, that of **prosopography** or collective biography. It is most often associated with the works of Sir Lewis Namier on the political class in eighteenth-century Britain, which has been continued and extended since his death by the History of Parliament Trust. Another important example is the work on the 'new class' of the early Roman Empire by Sir Ronald Syme. In prosopography the goal is to compile basic biographies for a large number of people who share some important feature in common. The aim is to see if there are any repeated features or patterns. This can be used to construct a biography of a 'typical' or archetypal member of the group and to see how this changes over time. It can also be used as the basis for a historical sociology and to explain why, on average, members of particular groups behaved in certain ways or were receptive to some ideas and not others. Most prosopography has also concentrated on elites, such as eighteenth-century politicians and Roman aristocrats, but it has been applied to other groups as, for example, in Olive Banks's study of feminist prosopography.[11]

One problematic aspect of biography is the role of **theory**, particularly psychological theories such as **psychoanalysis**. Peter Gay, in particular, has been a strong advocate of this in works such as *Freud for Historians* and throughout his other works more generally. There are some notable examples of this in biography, such as Eric Erickson's account of the young Martin Luther. However, the results have generally been disappointing, and have provoked sharp attacks from, among others, David Stannard and Jacques Barzun.[12] The problem from an empirical viewpoint is the constant danger of starting with a theory such as Freud's and then selecting those **facts** that will fit and confirm it. This problem is particularly serious when the theory does not yield testable **hypotheses**. In that case *any* fact can be fitted into the theory and made to support it. This means that it loses its explanatory power – by explaining everything it ends by explaining nothing. Even when this is not the case, there is still the problem for the empiricist of letting the theory direct and structure the research project and narrative. As we have seen before, for the empirical historian theories have use only after the work of research has started and are driven and trumped by facts rather then the other way around.

▶ Empirical historical biography – the case of Hitler

Empirical historical biography has become common since the early part of the twentieth century. To give some idea of its impact and success we can look at two examples. The first is one twentieth-century figure who has had more written about them than anyone else, that is Hitler. Much of what has been written about Hitler is not in any sense scholarly, and belongs to the realm of fiction or even outright fantasy.[13] However, since the 1960s there has been a succession of biographies which are evidence-based, follow cannons of scholarly practice, and are not driven by a present-minded agenda. What they reveal is an increase in understanding and knowledge, as the study of Hitler's life casts light not only on his career, but also on such questions as the nature and function of the Nazi state. This is not as easy as one might imagine: Hitler left few personal records as opposed to public ones and the memories and recollections of people who knew him have to be used with great caution. One consequence is that all the lives of Hitler are essentially political biography. To use the terminology given above, they concentrate on levels two and three. There were of course plentiful resources available for biographers from 1945 onwards. Over the years the amount of sources grew substantially, as more and more government and other documents became available. A series of publications made many German records more accessible, but the most significant breakthrough was the opening of the Russian archives after 1989. At the same time other studies, of the military and diplomatic history of World War II, of the Holocaust and of the Nazi party's rise to power, all clarified the meaning of many documents and increasingly raised new issues, particularly about the role played by Hitler in the Nazi state.

One of the first scholarly, comprehensive accounts of Hitler's life was Alan Bullock's *Hitler: A Study in Tyranny*, published in 1952. This reflects the sources available immediately after the war and was written before the many historiographical debates had started. As the sub-title suggests, the focus of the book is on Hitler as a despot, an absolute ruler, and it explores both how he was able to gain power, and his creation of a state dominated by one person – himself. In this view, Hitler was personally responsible for the principal events and policy decisions, even if these were carried out and executed by others. Bullock returned to the topic in *Hitler and Stalin: Parallel Lives* in 1991. This drew on both the many records that had become available since his first book and the historiographical debate which had started in the 1960s over the nature of the Nazi regime. Bullock continued to argue that the Nazi party was largely Hitler's personal creation and that its coming to power in 1933 would not have happened but for his political astuteness, even though circumstances and the error of others such as von Schleicher also played a part. He also argued that Hitler must have been directly responsible for the decision to launch the Final Solution, and that the intention to eliminate the Jewish population of Europe grew out of Hitler's longstanding anti-Semitism. He explicitly took account of the historiographical debate to amend his earlier picture of the Nazi state. Since the 1960s the picture had grown of the Third Reich as a bureaucratic chaos, with multiple, competing and overlapping authorities and jurisdictions and no clear lines of authority or responsibility. Bullock admitted this, but argued that Hitler was still the ultimate source of authority and decisions. This was because of the 'Hitler myth', of a charismatic and inspired leader, which gave him a unique authority and enabled him to act in an independent and arbitrary way, and also because of the existence of a parallel state, of institutions directly responsible to him, through which he could act in ways outside the law or other 'usual channels'. The SS was the most important of these, but not the only one.

Between 1952 and 1991 a number of other lives of Hitler had been published, of which the most important was Joachim Fest's *Hitler* published in 1973. This is a biography that concentrates very much on Hitler's personal role in events, and sees him as a person who was able to articulate and then control the collective crisis of German identity in the years after 1918. The most recent life is the monumental two-volume work of Kershaw, which marks a distinct advance on earlier interpretations. In the introduction to the first volume, *Hitler: Hubris*, Kershaw points out that as an institutionalist historian he was initially not persuaded that biography was a useful approach. However, his earlier work on Nazi Germany, *The Hitler Myth*, convinced him that to understand the policy of the German state, it was essential to study Hitler's personal role. The biography is much less focused on the actual personality of Hitler than either Fest's or Bullock's, and instead locates him within the web of organizations and institutions.[14] Kershaw uses recent research to amend Bullock's and Fest's pictures. He argues that Hitler was indeed the ultimate charismatic source of authority, but that this was often not exercised directly through orders transmitted downwards. Rather, many competing institutions and individuals sought to 'work towards the Führer' by taking actions which Hitler's previous announcements had led them to believe would gain his favour. This makes Hitler's ultimate responsibility for the Holocaust less clear (quite apart from the basic problem that there is no documentary evidence for this) and puts more weight on the role of figures such as Goering, Himmler and Heydrich.

▶ Empirical historical biography – the case of Gladstone

A very different figure who has also been the subject of several outstanding biographies is the British Liberal leader William Ewart Gladstone.[15] Unlike Hitler, Gladstone left a wealth of private papers, including an enormous correspondence and a daily journal which he kept for almost all of his adult life. He would seem an ideal subject for the biographer and has featured in several outstanding works. The most important early one was the *Life* by John Morley (1903). This was written with the benefit of personal knowledge, as Morley had been a close colleague and ally. Not surprisingly, it was also partisan and presented Gladstone in a consistently favourable light. Despite this, it was one of the best biographies of its kind. It was the starting point for all subsequent biographies until recently, such as the shorter one-volume work by Magnus (1954). Over the years certain issues clearly emerged in the historiography of Gladstone's career, including his relations with his Cabinet colleagues and the decision to opt for a policy of Irish Home Rule in 1885. In the last 20 years our understanding of these and other issues has been transformed by the use of Gladstone's private diaries, as well as much fuller use of his vast correspondence. This has found expression in two outstanding biographies by Colin Matthew and Richard Shannon. Mathew's work is a compilation of the introductions he wrote for the various volumes of the diaries. In it he clearly comes down on the pro-Gladstone side of the debates, arguing that he provided the essential leadership and sense of purpose to his governments and that he broadly supported and encouraged his Cabinet colleagues. He interprets the 'Hawarden Kite' (the episode in 1885 where Gladstone's move towards Irish Home Rule was made known to the press by his son, so precipitating a political crisis) and the whole split over Home Rule in a way that is favourable to Gladstone. He argues on the basis of the diaries and other evidence that Gladstone had been moving in this direction for some time and that it was ultimately a matter of principle for him. Shannon is more critical. He presents Gladstone as in many ways an erratic and difficult colleague and, while accepting that the 'Hawarden Kite' was not motivated by tactical political considerations, puts the blame for the subsequent split largely on Gladstone's shoulders rather than

Hartington's. What both of these lives show is the much greater insight historians now have into Gladstone's character and psychological state. Much more is also known now of the detailed political manoeuvrings at various critical points in his career. The debate now is over what gloss or 'spin' we should now put on this. What is certain is that older biographies, while useful, have been supplanted. Future discussion has to start with the work of Matthew and Shannon.

What the cases of both Hitler and Gladstone show is the way a strictly empirical approach to biography can lead to deeper knowledge and understanding of the individual and their place in history. We now know more about Gladstone's relations with the **Whigs** and the politics of Home Rule, and about the nature of the Nazi state and Hitler's role in it than we did 20 or 30 years ago. This is due to two things. First, more sources have become available. Second, and perhaps more significantly, the application of historical analysis to the empirical record has eliminated much unfounded speculation and increased our understanding of the evidence that was already available.

▶ Alternatives to empirical biography

There are of course other views of the form historical biography should take. Non-empirical biography, of lives told to inspire, or made to fit the demands of literary genres is still widespread. More complex are arguments taken from postmodernism and particularly the idea of 'microhistory', which derives ultimately from François Lyotard. The key idea here is the rejection of **'metanarrative'**, meaning any narrative that goes beyond the recounting of a single event. An account of an entire life which makes claims of being a 'true' one is regarded with scepticism for this reason, and also because it assumes a continuous and active identity on the part of the subject. Moreover, it means that the idea of a larger narrative into which an individual life fits and which gives the narrative of that life much of its meaning is also rejected. For Lyotard, all we can do is write fragmented accounts of single events. This could be the life of an individual or an account of an episode in the life of a person. Two well-known works which are seen as examples of this are *The Cheese and The Worms* by Carlo Ginzburg and *The Return of Martin Guerre* by Natalie Zemon-Davis. The first uses inquisition records to explore the mental world and beliefs of an Italian miller, while the second deals with an episode from the history of sixteenth-century France (well known today as the subject of an outstanding film).

Both concentrate on particular micro-events, are semi-biographical in that they deal with a significant aspect or a large part of the lives of individuals, and yet reject many of the conventions of empirical biography. This is particularly true in the case of Natalie Zemon-Davis. *The Return of Martin Guerre* contains a great deal, such as the description of the motives and character of Martin Guerre's wife, for which there is no empirical (that is, in this case, documentary) evidence. She defends this on the grounds that the picture she gives fits in with what we know about, for example, sixteenth-century French peasant society and the qualities of its womenfolk from other sources. However, in the book, the actual story is used to cast light on precisely such questions as the nature of marriage and the role of Protestantism in French society at that time. It is hard to do this when the narrative is, as Davis herself says, partly invented. Consequently, she has been severely criticized for this by other historians such as Richard Evans. Despite this, in both of these works the empirical historian keeps breaking through. Ginzburg explicitly locates his account in the wider narrative of social control and the pursuit of heresy in early modern Italy, while Davis's work is also based on very detailed empirical research into, for example, the career of Martin Guerre.[16]

Biography, despite the wariness with which many empiricist historians regard it, has remained a part of mainstream history, and as with other areas of history has benefited from the application of strict standards of evidence and inference. The rather chastening conclusion that many historians have come to, however, is that while the application of these methods may, as in the case of Hitler and Gladstone, lead to a real growth in our knowledge of historical figures and their historical significance, the number of people who can be looked at in this way is surprisingly small. The problem is simply lack of surviving records. Before the eighteenth century it is very unusual for even elite figures to leave a large body of record. The golden age for the biographer is certainly the period between about 1750 and 1920. This was a great age of letter writing and much of that correspondence has survived. By contrast, the twentieth century is much less well served. While historians have as much appreciation for the benefits of the telephone as anybody else does, they have a good reason to curse its invention in their professional capacity. By removing much of the need to write, it has eliminated the major source for the 'complete' biography. It may be that when strict standards of evidence are applied, biography can only play a major role in historiography for a limited period of the past. It is doubtful, though, that it will lose its appeal to either the public or the historian.

4 The Empirical History of Institutions

▶ The nature and importance of institutions

The history of institutions is where empirical history began, with the work of Alciato, Bodin and Baudoin in early modern France. It is also the area where the new professional historians of the nineteenth century had their greatest early triumphs. What, though, *is* institutional history or, to put it another way, what do we mean by an institution and in what way does it have a history?

The term 'institution' has two slightly different meanings. In the first sense institutions are social organizations that co-ordinate the activities of large numbers of people in order to achieve some common end or goal. Their most important feature is that this co-ordination is achieved not by force, but through a system of rules and organized or structured relations between the individuals involved. Typically, an institution will have one central function or 'product'. They are also typically hierarchical, that is, they have an internal structure and the relations between the individuals involved are organized through a hierarchy or system of ranks rather than by, for example, contracts. Examples of such institutions include the Church, the legal system, governments, business corporations, trades unions and universities.

As well as being hierarchical, institutions have another feature, one that makes them interesting and important for historians: they typically exist beyond the lifetimes of the individual human beings that make them up at any one time. So, an institution will have a history. Moreover, the history of an institution such as the Church or the Army, is more than just the collection of all of the biographies of the people who have composed it over time (important though this is). It also includes the history of the rules and structured relations between those individuals and the way they have changed over time.

Historians can find out about such matters because of another feature of institutions – they generate large amounts of records. These also tend to survive longer and in larger amounts than is the case with private records of the kind used in biography. The reason for this is simple: because institutions exist through time for more than the lifetime of any one individual, there are always people who have an interest in preserving the records of the past, which is not the case with private individuals. In fact, where the records of individual lives do survive, it is either because of accident or because they were connected to an institution of some kind. In some cases the actual function or purpose of the institution encourages the keeping of records so that the function can be carried out better; this is clearly the case with both law courts and universities for example.

The other use of the term 'institution' refers to a formal structure of rules that govern an activity or kind of interaction between human beings. It is in this sense that we speak of social institutions such as marriage or sport and organized games. This kind of institution will also have a history inasmuch as the rules and the practices that embody them have an origin and a story of development and transformations, which can be traced through time. The distinction between the two kinds of institution is not absolute. Some institutions such as the family or household fall into both categories and some recent thinkers would have it that structured relations are the principal feature of all institutions, of either kind.

Because institutions exist over relatively long spans of time and often generate copious records, it is possible to construct a history of an institution, whether it be the church, a business firm, or an institution of the state such as Parliament. The records tell us about the individual human beings who made up the institution, and about their interactions with each other and with those outside the institution. They also tell us about the rules that governed both of these sets of relations. As the records are produced through the course of time, we can use them to acquire knowledge that can then be used to construct a story, of the origins of the institution, the way it changed through time, became more complex, changed its function or acquired new ones, degenerated, and (sometimes) how it ceased to be. The most difficult part of this is typically that of establishing the origins of the institution. This is because institutions typically only start to generate large quantities of records once they have become established, so their earliest years are often shrouded in obscurity.

All this means that the history of institutions is possible. Why though *should* it be done, often in preference to (for example) biography or political history? The answer may seem obvious but is worth spelling out. The partial list of important institutions given earlier is a clue. It would be very difficult to imagine a meaningful history that did not touch on, or need to know about, some at least of those institutions. The appearance of organized institutions is one of the features of complex human societies, of civilizations. The absence of complex institutions is a common feature of societies that do not produce many records and are therefore difficult for historians to study. Moreover, the existence of many institutions, carrying out a wide range of functions, is one of the most prominent features of our world, the one that we inhabit. Clearly also, in any historical period and for most parts of the world the nature of the society at any given time and its history up to that point can only be understood if one has a grasp of the history and nature of its principal institutions.

▶ Empirical history and institutions

Institutional history is the area where, until very recently, the dominance of the empirical approach was most marked. There has not been an alternative model, as in biography, nor a relationship with a body of abstract **theory**, as in economic history. The reasons for this are partly accidental: most of the theoretical thinking about organizations and institutions has been done by disciplines such as management and sociology, which have had relatively little impact on historians. However, it also reflects something deeper.

Institutions do not just produce voluminous records, which clearly make the task of the historian much easier. They also produce records of a particular kind, formulaic, highly structured and full of technical terms that mean something to an insider but little to anyone else. They are very different from the kinds of records produced by people acting in their personal capacity, or small businesses. Records of this kind contain great quantities of information. However, they can only be understood, and the information they contain be extracted, by applying the kind of analytical techniques discussed earlier in Chapter 2. Institutions create records that make empirical history much easier, but they also make the techniques of empirical history necessary if one is to fully understand them. One important aspect of this is that much of the information the records contain is, in Marwick's terminology, '**unwitting**', that is, it has nothing to do with the original intent of the writer or with the original function of the text.[1] A tax record can tell us many things about, for example, the social divisions in society, the nature of wealth and what was considered valuable at a given time, none of which the original author was intending to record.

The nature of institutional records also means that knowledge can expand as study leads to greater understanding. Study of the records leads to greater understanding of the institution and its history. This in turn leads to greater understanding of the documents so that features of the records which were not understood or even not noticed before now become meaningful. The result is a positive feedback or virtuous circle of increasing knowledge, at least for a time (after a while the returns from research diminish as the institution is fully understood).

As we have already seen, institutional history (mainly of law) was the starting point for empirical history. Looking at the **historiography** of institutions reveals a clear pattern to the story of historians' understanding of them. This pattern is also found in most empirical historical research over time, but is often easier to discern in institutional history. The starting point is the traditional understanding of the institution, which is frequently a matter of **myth** or folk memory and tradition rather than real knowledge. The next stage is **antiquarian** research, which clarifies what records exist and which ones are reliable. From this comes a more coherent **narrative**. However, the narrative so produced is based on research but lacks proper use of the **sources**, and in particular does not distinguish sufficiently between original and later records. This means that much of the myth survives (much of this antiquarian research is intended to support the mythical account) and that there is a problem of **anachronism**, with earlier forms of the institution being treated as though they were like their later versions. However, the original work makes clear where there are problems in the records. A problem of interpretation is identified or a question is formulated. This leads to document- and record-based research using proper critical techniques. This in turn casts doubt on aspects of the original narrative, which has to be amended. It also throws up new questions and opens up new topics of research. Over time the questions become more narrowly focused and come to deal with finer points of detail. Eventually, more and more of the account is in the realm of the consensus or the generally agreed. However, there is often also a problem, inasmuch as the detailed and specific knowledge accumulated by the end of this process tends to overwhelm the narrative structure that gives it meaning, resulting in many detailed studies of particular aspects of the institution or of specific episodes in its history but no real overall story. As the next chapter also shows, this is a recurring difficulty with empirical historiography in many areas.

In the area of institutional history empiricism leads to a historiography with specific qualities, just as it does in biography. Obviously, like all historiography of this type, it will aim to be strictly evidence-based and to eschew unsupported assertions. This means that myths of origin are frequently cast aside as unfounded. The intention, even if it is seen as impossible to fully realize, is to establish as far as possible what exactly can be said with confidence about the origins of the institution and its nature at various stages of its history, rather than to 'create' an account or narrative of it. The focus is upon the human rather than the super-natural, and on the concrete, mundane and typical rather than the extraordinary or unusual. So, for example, a history of the criminal justice system would concentrate on how the institutions dealt with ordinary, average crimes such as theft rather than looking at spectacular crimes such as gory murders or serial killers.

One of the main aims in history of this type is to avoid a specific form of anachronism. This is the tendency to assume that because an institution has certain qualities, or works in a particular way at one time in its history, it has always been like that. This can lead to reading features of the present of an institution into its past or to seeing it as timeless and unchanging rather than as historical. Lawyers are particularly prone to see their own institutions in this way but the same is true of other professions – including academics! So, in empirical institutional history the emphasis is on change and development through time as well as continuity. There is a concentration on the institution itself, its rules, procedures and structure, rather than on individual personalities or instances. A history of Parliament will look at things like the evolution of Parliament's role in government, the rules governing elections, and procedures rather than the foibles of particular individual MPs. Finally, the notion that has to be avoided at all costs is what is usually known as '**Whig**' **history** of the institution. This refers to the habit of seeing the evolution of an institution as being somehow intended to produce its state at the time the historian is writing. This state of affairs is typically seen as the perfected (or almost perfected) outcome of the historical process. To think this way means that past forms of the institution are judged or described not on their own terms, but as imperfect approximations of the later form they were moving towards. This is known as 'Whig' history because it was the distinctive feature of an account of the British constitution that was closely associated with that political party. This way of doing institutional history can still be found today and is especially common in histories of the welfare state.[2]

▶ Ecclesiastical history

The two topics where empirical institutional history began were ecclesiastical and legal history. The origins of ecclesiastical history lie back in the world of late antiquity, with the fourth-century *Ecclesiastical History* of Eusebius. However this tradition died away during the Middle Ages, like so much else in ancient historiography, and was replaced largely by lives of saints and eminent churchmen, and by apocalyptic works that tried to use the length of time the Church had existed as a clue to how near the apocalypse might be. As with legal history, it was the early modern period that saw a more empirical approach to Church history, due to the impact of humanism and the religious disputes of the time. The most significant product of this time was the *History of the Council of Trent* (1619) by Paolo Sarpi (1552–1623) which gave a generally critical view of the Council, even though Sarpi was nominally a Catholic.

However, it was the seventeenth century that saw the real advent of documentary studies in this area, with the work of the **Maurists** and the Bollandists. We have already had occasion to mention the Maurists for their general contribution to empirical study of the past through their work on **diplomatics**. They were particularly interested in the history of a sub-institution of the Church, the religious orders, especially their own. The Bollandists were an offshoot of the Jesuit order, founded in the early seventeenth century and still in existence after being refounded in 1857. Their work, still not yet complete, was to compile a scholarly edition of all of the lives of the saints of the Catholic calendar, the *Acta Sanctorum*. This is an example of how the initial impetus for research is to confirm traditional legends. It also shows how such work can lead to unexpected discoveries – the Bollandists' critical editions of saints' lives are an important source for many periods, due to the extensive **unwitting testimony** they contain about the intellectual and social conditions of the times when they were written.

Ecclesiastical history was one of the first areas that the new Rankean historians turned their attention to. Much of this centred on the principal office of the Catholic Church, the Papacy. Two of the early workers in this particular vineyard were the German scholar Ludwig von Pastor (1854–1928) and his English counterpart Mandell Creighton (1843–1901) (himself a bishop). They certainly produced in bulk: Pastor's *History of the Popes* ran to 40 volumes between 1886 and 1933, while Creighton managed a respectable five volumes for his *History of the Papacy During the Period of the Reformation* (1882–94). One important feature of these works, particularly Creighton's, was their deliberate attempt to write dispassionate, disinterested history in the Rankean mode, in an area where much of the writing was passionate advocacy and polemic. In Creighton's case this aroused the ire of Lord Acton, who accused him of eschewing moral judgement in a reprehensible way.

As well as trying to remove much of the polemic from the study of this area, historians such as Creighton and Pastor moved the focus away from the biographical details of the Church, that is the lives of individual Popes (although obviously there was still a good deal of this in their work). They looked at the office itself, rather than its holders, and began to develop an understanding of how the Papacy had evolved and changed over time. This counteracted the tendency, common until then, to read the powerful and effective Papacy of the high Middle Ages backwards into earlier periods. There was also an increasing emphasis on the growth of other parts of the Church, particularly the curia or central administration.

The next phase was the work of several twentieth-century historians but above all of Fliche (1884–1951). In three books published between 1924 and 1937, he created what became the dominant interpretation of the medieval Church, that there had been a radical change in the organization and nature of its institutions during the twelfth century. He invented the term that is usually used to describe this movement, the 'Gregorian Reform' (after its leading figure Pope Gregory VII).[3] He was also responsible along with Victor Martin for editing and organizing the 21-volume *Histoire de L'Église* (1934–52), which remains even now the best study of the overall course of Church history. In recent years the history of the Reformation and post-Reformation Church has been transformed, but the older history of the medieval Church, while challenged, remains largely intact. This however reflects the relative lack of interest in the topic.

▶ The origins of legal history

As we saw earlier, legal history was the area where a truly historical perspective first developed, due to the work of men like Alciato and Bodin. The movement in the eighteenth century was away from a notion of the origins of law and the legal system that was either religious or based on the idea of a 'legislator' or law creator.

This was a controversial process and not simple. The origin of law was one of the interests of the speculative histories of the Enlightenment, with a search for an origin in the nature of the world or of human beings rather than in divine instruction or design. (This approach made use of the theological idea of 'natural law', but removed or greatly diminished the element of divine purpose that had originally been part of it.) This theoretical history came to be linked with the later eighteenth-century critique of the existing legal system in the writings of legal reformers such as Cesare Beccaria and, above all, Jeremy Bentham. From Bentham and his followers came the idea of law as a defined and designed code or system of rules, produced by the sovereign power of the state to achieve certain ends, such as 'the greatest possible happiness of the greatest possible number'. Bentham and his followers in Britain and on the Continent called for the creation of a rationally designed code, which would replace the existing system of law. This idea gained further support with the concrete example of the creation of the Code Napoleon in France. This was a radically ahistorical view of what law was or should be. It, and the programme it inspired, was also deeply controversial.

It was of course controversial for a number of reasons. The kind of reforms advocated by legal reformers involved sweeping away many old institutions. They also posed a threat to established interests among the upper classes and the legal profession. It was also controversial because it ran directly against the work of the new historians of those old institutions. They were abandoning the idea that law had either been handed down by God or created wholesale by a single legislator such as the legendary figures of Solon or Lycurgus in ancient Greece. Instead, it was seen as the outcome of a process of evolution and accretion, even if individual kings had played a part in creating it. Now reformers such as Bentham were arguing that while law may have been like this in the past, this only confirmed its irrationality and confusion: now was the time to replace tradition and history with reason. This went against the thinking about legal institutions and law brought about by their historical study.

This was the context in which in 1814 the German author A. F. Thibault published a work calling for a general codification of German law on Napoleonic lines. The response came swiftly, the same year in fact, from Friedrich Carl von Savigny (1779–1861). Savigny was a distinguished lawyer, who held the chair of Roman law at several universities, culminating in Berlin where he was professor from 1810 to 1842. He opposed the ahistorical argument of the philosophers by asserting that law was a historical institution, the meaning of which was a product of its growth over time. This in turn was not the result of any person's will but rather an organic, incremental process, reflecting historical circumstances and events and the '*Volksgeist*' or spirit of the people. This meant that in order to truly understand the institutions of the legal system, including the law itself, you had to study its history, employing empirical methods.

Savigny himself undertook this research into the historical origins and development of European law, as part of the controversy over codification which went on for many years. As this happened at the same time that Ranke and others were creating the modern discipline of academic history the result was a great surge of interest by historians in the topic. Savigny himself played a significant part in this with a six-volume history of Roman law in the Middle Ages. This marked a major advance on the work of the Renaissance legal scholars, inasmuch as Savigny tried with some success to trace the actual story of the process by which the Roman law had been transformed and adapted to become the *jus commune* of late medieval and early modern Europe. This meant looking at the history of Roman law after the end of the Roman state, rather than trying to reconstruct the actual law of Rome itself as Alciato and others had done. He tended to see legal institutions as the product of culture and so concentrated on lawyers, teachers and theorists, rather than on the social and political context of law or the structure of the courts.[4]

The history of legal institutions began, then, in the heat of a political controversy. The initial work had been done before Savigny, in the work of the German historian Justus Moser (1720–1794). His *History of Osnabruck* introduced the main features of institutional history using empirical research. He was followed by a number of historians besides Savigny, of whom the most important was Georg von Maurer (1790–1872). At this point, in the early nineteenth century, the dominant accounts of the history of legal institutions were at the first stage described earlier. They relied upon antiquarian research and put forward a narrative that was still largely based on tradition. There were in fact two such narratives. One traced the institutions of most European nations, including the law, back to the Germanic tribes that had occupied the western provinces of the Roman Empire during the fifth and sixth centuries. In this view most of the traditional legal and constitutional institutions of Europe originated in free self-governing communities of Germanic peasant freeholders or '*Markgenossenschaften*' as Moser had called them. The other, initially a minority view, argued for the continuing influence of Roman forms and institutions, even after the disappearance of the Roman state.

The work of investigating the newly available archives of the old legal and other institutions was taken up by the first generation of professional historians in Germany and spread from there to other countries. Important early figures were Otto von Gierke (1841–1921) and Heinrich Brunner (1840–1915). Brunner's great work was the *History of German Law* (1887/92), which argued for the influence of late Roman law on medieval German legal institutions. Gierke investigated the important legal institution of the corporate person and traced its origins back to the medieval Church and town.

Over the next hundred years the research came to focus on a number of issues, some of which are still open. Legal history tended for obvious reasons to focus on the development of national legal systems, but there was a continuing interest in comparisons between different countries. In England the crucial figures were firstly the Russian émigré Paul Vinogradoff (1854–1925), who became professor of jurisprudence at Oxford in 1903 and set up a seminar on the Rankean model, which produced many outstanding medievalists. He had already made important contributions to English legal history in *Villainage in England* (1892).[5] The other was the man who is often regarded as the greatest historian that England has ever produced, Frederick William Maitland (1850–1906).

Maitland was originally not a historian but a barrister. He found his *metier* after being introduced to legal history by Vinogradoff in 1883. His masterpiece is the *History of English Law to the Time of Edward I* (1895). (This work is almost entirely Maitland's, despite Sir Frederick Pollock's appearance as co-author.) In this book Maitland achieved a very rare feat in the world of historiography. He produced a book that was immediately seen as definitive for its subject and which has still not been challenged in any of its main arguments over a hundred years later. This was done on the basis of a strictly empirical method. Maitland swept away the remnants of the traditional view of the origins of English law and constructed an analytical account based on **primary sources**, many of which he edited for the Selden Society. He demonstrated the primarily Saxon origins of English law, the limited effect (in this area) of the Norman Conquest, and the central part played in the appearance of the English legal system by the reforms of Henry II and Edward I. Most of the book gives an account of the law and its institutions in Angevin England and makes clear the enormous complexity of the system without simplifying it. Most subsequent legal history in England has built on Maitland's foundations. The most significant work to follow his was the *Concise History of the Common Law* (1929) by T. F. T. Plucknett. In recent years the principal works are J. H. Baker's *An Introduction to English Legal History* (1979) and *Historical Foundations of the Common Law* (1969) by S. F. C. Milsom.[6]

One of the earliest debates among scholars was the one alluded to above, over the relative importance of Roman and Germanic sources for various institutions. Initially, the Germanic model was predominant but it came under increasing attack, as the empirical evidence of sources such as legal and official documents proved not to support it. In France this assault was led by Fustel de Coulanges via his massive work *Histoire des Institutions Politiques de L'Ancienne France* (1874–89). He argued that in France there had been no abrupt change from the Roman period to the Merovingians and that most of the institutions of the medieval French state could be traced back to the later Roman period. In particular he argued that the institutions that later became what we call 'feudalism' were already starting to appear in the fourth and fifth centuries. At the time these ideas were very controversial, but Fustel based them on massive documentary research and later work has tended to confirm his arguments.

In England a position similar to Fustel's was taken by Frederic Seebohm (1833–1912). In *The English Village Community* (1883) he argued like Fustel that the medieval institutions of the manor and villainage (servile landholding by peasants) had originated in the Roman villa. He was able to do great damage to the notion of free Saxon village communities as the source of English institutions, but many of his arguments were themselves overthrown by the later empirical work of Vinogradoff and Maitland. This and other research led to the conclusion that while Roman survivals played a large role in the institutional history of continental Europe, they had only a walk-on part in England.

▶ Constitutional history – the fall of the Whigs

As the history of legal institutions progressed it led naturally to an interest in constitutional history, the history of the totality of the institutions of government and of the rules which regulate the working of the political system. This was natural because the determination and enforcement of law is one of the central functions of government. Study of the law inevitably meant the study of the institutions that created and defined it. In the English case, for example, the study of medieval law logically implied the study of Parliament. The period between 1850 and 1930 was the great age of constitutional history. Much of the effort was devoted to uncovering the foundations or origins of national constitutions rather than their later, better known development. In Germany this took the form of exploring the complex constitution of the medieval Holy Roman Empire, while in France researchers looked at the institutions of the Capetian monarchy and the origins of bodies such as the Estates General.

As with legal history, constitutional history sprang out of political controversy. This was very much the case in Britain where interest in the subject came about partly because of the many disputes over constitutional reform during the later eighteenth and early nineteenth centuries. The history of the English constitution clearly demonstrates the impact that empirical methods had on this kind of topic. In the first place there is the huge initial role of myth and tradition, coupled with narratives constructed for partisan reasons. From the seventeenth century onwards, there was the notion of the 'ancient constitution' which traced English political institutions back to the Anglo-Saxon period. This idea of a 'Gothick' constitution was a favourite of radicals from the seventeenth century onwards. During the period of the Civil War, antiquarian research into Parliament's origins and powers by figures such as Denzil Holles and William Prynne was used to support the claims of Parliament against both Charles I and Cromwell.[7]

During the eighteenth century, radicals and opponents of the Whig governments after 1715 used this kind of antiquarian research to claim that Walpole and his successors had undermined and corrupted the true old constitution through bribery and manipulation of the franchise. Some Whigs in turn employed similar arguments after the accession of George III, while Tories and Jacobites both had their own accounts of English constitutional history. All of these accounts rested on antiquarian works on Parliamentary enactments and precedents, the authority and franchises of burghs as defined by their charters (important because this determined how their Parliamentary representatives were selected), and a romantic history of early medieval England. The main points of disagreement between Whig, radical and Tory accounts were over the relations between the various parts of the constitution (particularly Crown, Lords and Commons) and the meaning and interpretation of the events of the seventeenth century, especially the Revolution of 1688.

The early nineteenth century demonstrates the second feature of the process, the creation of a sounder version of the traditional narrative. The main person responsible was Henry Hallam (1777–1859). In 1827 he published *The Constitutional History of England from the Accession of Henry VII to the Death of George II*, intended to demolish Hume's Tory account of the seventeenth century. He argued that the Tudors had undermined, and the Stuarts had intended to destroy, the established constitution, which he identified with the picture given by the traditional accounts. He argued further that the Glorious Revolution had perfected English government. His view therefore was Whig, but of a very moderate kind. The more thoroughgoing Whig account came in the pages of the *History of England* by T. B. Macaulay.[8]

At this point many of the most important primary sources for the history of medieval political institutions were inaccessible. This began to change from the 1840s onwards and a key event in this process was the publication in 1870 of *Select Charters and Other Documents Illustrative of English History* by William Stubbs. With these and other manuscript sources becoming available, it became possible to apply techniques of empirical research and to move beyond the traditional account sketched out by Hallam. Stubbs himself undertook this task with the three-volume *Constitutional History of Medieval England* (1873–8). This was the first real attempt to write a history of the political institutions of medieval England from original sources. The method and approach was taken from the new historical scholarship in Germany and the most influential model was the monumental *Deutsche Verfassungsgeschichte* (1844–78) of Georg Waitz

Much of the myth was now dispelled, but the narrative produced by Stubbs came in for criticism itself, on the basis of the sources he himself had made available. His account of the Angevin period withstood this, and remains broadly in place, but his views of the Saxon and Norman periods were replaced, as was his general approach. Although a Tory himself, he presented a classic 'Whig' account of constitutional history. In this way of thinking the system of parliamentary government created by the 1832 Reform Act was as close to perfection as was possible and the whole of English constitutional history was essentially the slow process by which that government had emerged from earlier, imperfect forms. The origins were seen to lie in the Saxon past – Stubbs was very much on the Germanist side of the debate described above – with the Saxon Witanegemot as the original from which Parliament had grown. An even more strongly 'Saxonist' account was given by Stubbs's contemporary E. A. Freeman. Freeman's work was not as soundly based as Stubbs's, because it made no use of manuscript sources such as charters and depended instead on chronicle evidence of dubious reliability.[9]

Several scholars carried out the work that ultimately recast Stubbs's narrative. The most important was J. H. Round (1854–1928) but others such as Maitland were also significant. The principal issues were the date and manner of the introduction of feudalism into England, the nature of early representative institutions, the impact of 1066 on law and government, and the origin of Parliament. Some of these debates are still 'live', such as the still-vexed issue of how far the Normans introduced any significant legal and institutional innovations. Others are now closed with an established consensus. Nobody now believes that the Saxon Witan was the original source of the later Parliament, the critical importance for many institutions of the reign of Henry II is accepted. (Maitland described this by saying that for English history, 1166 was more important than 1066.) Of the traditional idea of the 'ancient constitution', almost nothing is left.

▶ Administrative history

After the more detailed debate and the gradual replacement of the traditional narrative by one based on evidence came the next stage, the opening up of new but related areas of enquiry. In the case of England this took the form of a growing interest in administrative institutions such as the exchequer and household government. Again, this was made possible by the publication, calendarization and editing of primary sources, such as pipe rolls (these are medieval Treasury records). The pioneering work here was done by T. F. Tout (1855–1929) in his *Chapters in the Administrative History of Medieval England* (1920–31), which used original records to look at the day-to-day workings of medieval administration through institutions such as the exchequer, chancery and wardrobe. One of his discoveries, explored by later historians, was the way successive kings had moved the centre of administration from one office to another as each in turn fell under the control of feudal magnates, with the original dominant office becoming a ceremonial sinecure while the real business was carried on elsewhere.

The constitutional and administrative history of England after the Middle Ages has proved less difficult but there has still been debate. In the Tudor period this has centred round the supposed *Tudor Revolution in Government* as proposed by Geoffrey Elton. According to this thesis there was a radical transformation of English government during the 1530s, brought about by Henry VIII's minister Thomas Cromwell. Elton based his argument on the evidence of the state papers of Henry's reign and used these to attack the older view of Tudor monarchy put forward by A. F. Pollard (1869–1948). The thesis he put forward was then, in typical fashion, subjected to attack. It subsequently enjoyed a revival before suffering once more, largely at the hands of Elton's pupils. The other principal debate in this period was over the nature and role of Parliaments during the Tudor period, particularly during the reign of Elizabeth. The constitutional history of the seventeenth and eighteenth centuries has been largely subsumed within the political history of that period (see Chapter 5 below).[10]

▶ The history of the family and household – an empirical success story

Two other examples of institutional history illustrate both the way that empirical research works in this area and the impact of other approaches. The first is the history of the most important of the second kind of institution described above, those of marriage and the family. The institutional history of the household has attracted a great deal of attention, and experienced a revolutionary breakthrough in recent years.[11] In the past, family and household structure were simply taken for granted or seen as timeless and unchanging. This began to change in the nineteenth century, due to the scale of the social changes taking place then which made people more aware of the historicity of such institutions.

The pioneer in this area was the French sociologist Frederic le Play. On the basis of work in various regions of France, he identified three kinds of household and family structure. These were the nuclear family where the household consisted of a married couple and their unmarried children, the extended family where the household contained several generations, and the stem family where the household was made up of a married couple and their oldest male child and his spouse and children. All of these household structures reflected a set of rules (an institution) governing such matters as courtship, marriage and, most importantly, the question of whether or not people left the family household on being married. This was a sociological analysis, but le Play gave it an historical dimension.

He did this by arguing that the extended household had been the typical or dominant form of pre-industrial European society but had been displaced by the nuclear form during the process of industrialization. This remained the dominant perception of the history of the family for many years. Another important supposition was that in medieval and early modern Europe people had typically married at an early age. Neither of these beliefs was founded on real empirical evidence. The one about age of marriage was derived principally from literary evidence. The argument about household structure came from a conservative perception of industrialization as a destructive force that had destroyed a more organic and natural past, with which the extended household was identified.

The problem was that there seemed to be no easy way of discovering empirically how the institution of the household had worked or been structured in the past. The only individual cases for which there were extensive records were royal and aristocratic households, which were by definition unrepresentative. The break-through came in the 1950s with the work of the French demographer Louis Henry. He developed a standardized method for what was called 'family reconstitution'. This was done by using the registers of baptisms, marriages and deaths kept throughout Western Europe from the sixteenth century onwards. By matching up names in the different registers, it was possible to construct a kind of genealogy that traced the formation, composition and dissolution of households over time. When Henry invented this technique the computer was not available for historical research, and so the process had to be done laboriously by hand.

In Britain the first person to use it was E. A. Wrigley in his study of the parish of Colyton in Devon. Later, Peter Laslett organized the Cambridge Group for the Study of Population and a series of historical demographic studies were carried out. The results, summarized in works such as *Household and Family in Past Time* (1972), completely overthrew the older perspective. It became clear that the nuclear family had been the predominant type over most of Western Europe as far back as there were adequate records for family reconstitution. (Other records, now looked at in a different light, suggest that this was the case from at least the twelfth century.) It also became clear that the age of marriage was much older than had been thought, being usually in the mid- to late twenties. All this demonstrates how the use of the evidence left by the past (that is, empirical research) can bring about a dramatic growth in knowledge. This also engendered further debate over issues that were not so clear, such as the extent of population mobility before industrialization and the extent to which contraception was practised. In these areas the evidence was suggestive, but not conclusive.[12]

▶ The history of family relations

As well as examining the structure of the household, historians became interested in the internal organization of the institution, that is, the pattern of relations between the members of households and the rules and expectations that governed them. Two issues soon became prominent: the nature of the marital relationship and the relation between parents and children. The early work on these subjects was done by a number of historians, such as Edward Shorter, Lloyd Demause, Lawrence Stone and Phillippe Aries. Their work was strongly influenced by a number of theoretical approaches, particularly by **psychoanalysis**. The view that emerged had a number of features, the most prominent being that the concept of childhood as a state distinct from adulthood did not emerge until the eighteenth or nineteenth century, and that relations between spouses, and parents and children were generally cold and lacking in affection before the modern period.

These views have been sharply attacked and, particularly in the case of attitudes towards children, effectively demolished by later empirical work, most notably that of Stephen Ozment and Linda Pollock. Pollock pointed out that the arguments made by the earlier historians were theory driven and did not rest on empirical evidence. Where original sources were used, the problem was their atypical and unrepresentative nature. Her own and Ozment's work corrected this by using records that were commonplace and ordinary.[13] There has been less work done on marriage as an institution, despite its importance. The work that is being done emphasizes the extent to which the rigorous strict enforcement of laws about marriage is relatively recent. However, the exploration of such matters as 'irregular' (that is, non-standard) marriage and folk-divorce through practices such as wife sale, is continuing despite being hampered by the lack of surviving evidence.

▶ History of criminal law and punishment

Another area that has seen much research in recent years is the institutions of the criminal law and its enforcement. This aspect of legal history was neglected for many years, but has seen a substantial growth more recently. Much of this belongs to social rather than institutional history. There is still, however, an acute interest in the nature and development of some of the elements of the criminal justice system, particularly the police force and the prison. The 'early definitive' work for England is certainly the *History of English Criminal Law and its Administration Since 1750* (1948–56) by Sir Leon Radzinowicz. This makes use of a wide range of official records, particularly parliamentary papers and government publications, while also drawing on contemporary pamphlets and other literature. The account that it gives is one which reflects the views of earlier legal reformers: the older system of law enforcement is seen as ineffective and its transformation by a series of reforms as an example of enlightened administration. In particular, the creation of a publicly funded police force is seen as both necessary and desirable.

The research done more recently by scholars such as Peter King, Robert Storch and Clive Emsley has begun to lead to a questioning of this picture and we are now getting a series of works which look at the creation and practice of the police as an institution. Meanwhile, the actual workings of the old system have been explored by a number of authors, John Beattie being the most notable of these. This has started a number of debates. One of the most interesting centred on the work of Douglas Hay. Research had confirmed that the number of capital crimes had risen sharply during the eighteenth century, while the number of actual executions had remained stable or even declined. Hay explained this by arguing that the legal system played a key role in sustaining the ideological dominance of the ruling class through creating a myth of equality before the law and benevolence on the part of the elite. In two articles, John Langbein and Peter King were able to show that the empirical evidence of the court records did not support Hay's argument. Langbein pointed out that Hay's model was an example of an undisprovable theory, which could incorporate any evidence. He also pointed out that Radzinowicz's work contained an explanation of the evidence which was both simpler and testable.

The other institution connected to the criminal law that has attracted much attention is the prison. Again there is a traditional account, one which emphasizes a story of progressive reform. Here, however, much of the initial impetus for research has come from an author whose work encapsulates a quite different approach to the study of institutions as compared to the empirical one, Michel Foucault. His work on institutions derives from his wider argument about power relations in society and the way these determine both what can be known and how it is known. For Foucault, the distinction made earlier between different types of institution is otiose. All institutions are structures of power and domination that control the people who participate in them. This approach lends itself to the study of the prison, which he undertook in one of his best known works *Discipline and Punish* (1979). This looked at the new institution of the prison as it emerged in the early nineteenth century as the embodiment of a new kind of power order that was emerging at that time. (In other works he also examined other institutions such as the clinic and the asylum.)

This was a quite different approach. For a while it was very influential, but the centre of gravity of the historical profession has reasserted itself. More recent work on the prison as an institution is firmly empirical, looking at the writings of prison reformers and the administrative records produced by prison systems to construct an account of the origins of the institution, intellectual and administrative, and the way it has functioned in reality since its appearance. Theories that were once influential, such as Foucault's or the notion of 'social control', and were derived from sociology, feature much less prominently than was the case even ten years ago. The emphasis now is on the prison as an historically located institution with a specific origin and an institutional history of the kind described earlier.[14]

Institutional history, then, is a topic that lacks the drama of political history or the human interest of biography. It is, however, crucial for our understanding of several other aspects of the human past. The nature of institutional records and the need to establish a coherent narrative of the history of institutions in order to fully understand them mean that while other approaches bring valuable insights, the empirical one is likely to remain the dominant one. However, the historiography of institutions also reveals something else, that is, the way in which the cycle of empirical research described earlier tends to undermine the narrative that makes sense of an otherwise chaotic mass of discrete facts. The large-scale narratives of English constitutional history produced by earlier authors such as Stubbs had a clear structure, the growth of free government, into which the detailed facts could be fitted. As later authors such as Round and Plucknett did their work, much more became known about the specifics, but the larger picture became hard to discern under all of the detail. Eventually, the larger narrative tended to vanish in much work and all that was left was a rather antiquarian study of specific government bodies. This problem is a recurring one in empirical historiography, and can be seen very clearly in our next topic, political history.

5 Political History – The Master Topic?

► **What Is political history?**

Political history, like biography, is a form of **historiography** that has been around for a very long time, ever since Thucydides first set out to write a history of the Peloponnesian War.[1] It resembles historical biography in another way: the nature of both has been altered by the advent of empirical history. As with the other areas we have looked at, the empirical approach produces a distinctive way of examining the subject of political history. This is obscured to some degree by the persistence of other, older ways of approaching it – another parallel. Political history is often seen as the type of empirical history *par excellence*, even more so than institutional history. This is not actually true in **theory**, but the practice lends weight to this argument. Much mainstream historiography is both empirical in theory and method, and dominated by politics as its subject matter. Moreover, the most aggressively self-conscious empirical historians, such as Elton, are also identified with the case for political history as the primary or central area for historical research and investigation. This focus on political history is partly itself a historical phenomenon, reflecting both the way the historical profession grew up and the background of many of its early members. It also reflects something about the kind of concerns that an empirical approach brings and the way this leads to concentration on certain areas of the past. This can be seen from the way that the argument over the predominance of political history keeps on recurring. There have been several attempts to dethrone political history from its leading position, which have enjoyed some success for a while, but eventually there is a movement back.

As with institutional history, it is important to be clear what political history is. Only if we are clear about this can we understand what it is that historians are trying to do. This may seem a simple matter; political history is the history of politics. That is to say, it is the history of the political process in a given political entity and of the actors involved in it. Unfolding this definition reveals just how wide-ranging and complex a subject this is. The concern with human actors (or 'subjects' in the current modish jargon) means that it has a definite biographical element. All political history of this sort is concerned with the actions and choices of individual men and women, even if they are acting within a specific historical context.

76

On the other hand, political history is not purely biographical. It is also concerned with people in the mass or collective, with people as members of groups or classes. Above all, it is concerned with the political process itself, with the structures and rules within which politics takes place. To make an analogy, the study of an organized sport is not only a matter of recording the content and outcome of particular matches or the part played in these events by individual stars. It is also about the rules governing the sport, the way these have changed and evolved, and the way they broadly determine the shape that the game takes when actually played. Similarly, political history looks at the nature of the rules and expectations, the social and institutional structures within which political actors operate and the way these change over time. A study of politics in the Middle Ages will be concerned with the character, aspirations and decisions of individual monarchs, but it will also look at the nature of the office of monarchy and the systems of rules and governance through which those rulers had to work.

Political history therefore, while it has a biographical element, is about the history of political systems and institutions. This gives it a close connection to institutional history. Indeed, many important works can be put into either category and there is no clear-cut division. On the other hand, there are some works that are clearly of one type and some of the other. To give an example, a history of the medieval Papacy that concentrated on the competition for power within the curia and the College of Cardinals, and on the Papacy's relations with other states, would clearly belong to the genre of political history, while one which emphasized the rules and practices governing the Papacy, and such matters as the system of canon law, would just as clearly fall under the heading of administrative history.

The example just given also illustrates something else about political history. It is concerned with tracing not only the workings of the political process, but the subject matter of that process. This, in two words, is power and conflict. Lenin once observed that the crucial question in politics was 'Who/Whom' – who did things and to whom were they done? The ultimate question of politics is that of where power lies and how it is used. The questions that have to be put are: Who has the power? How is it acquired? How is it employed and what disagreements arise over this? Most historians of politics espouse (whether they know it or not) what is known as the **conflict theory of politics** (as opposed to its opposite, the **consensus theory**). This holds that divisions and clashes of interest in society are natural and inevitable. Politics is the process by which these clashes are resolved. This does not mean that politics is at base a kind of Hobbesian state of nature or war of all against all. On the contrary, it is a rule-bound process that works to prevent conflict from getting out of control. The outcome of politics is that groups with conflicting interests arrive at some kind of *modus vivendi*. This may be very much to the benefit of one group rather than another, but this is not the same as armed strife. The historian of politics is concerned to trace who has power and how that power shifts over time, how conflicts arise and how they are resolved.

One common conclusion is that political history is inevitably a history of elites, apart from rare occasions, such as revolutions and rebellions, when the lower orders rudely burst onto the stage. In practice this has a great element of truth in it, but this is not an inevitable feature of political history. Historians of politics tend to focus on elites for two reasons. The first is simply that in this, as in other areas of life, the elite leaves more records. The second, more profound reason, is this: in all societies of which we have record, power is unequally distributed, so that we can speak of a power elite. The decisions made by these people and the divisions among them will have much greater consequences. This makes them more interesting to historians.

However, the mass of the population in any society, the subaltern classes as they are sometimes called, are not mere extras on the stage of politics and serious political history has to pay attention to them. David Hume pointed out that all political orders are founded ultimately upon opinion. By this he meant that no matter how powerful the instruments of force at the disposal of rulers may be, they are always outnumbered by the sheer mass of the ruled. Ruling elites therefore are always ultimately constrained by a passive veto on the part of the public in general: there are always limits to what they can actually do. One of the tasks of the true political historian is to try and discern where those limits were at any time. This also means paying attention to forms of popular protest and resistance such as riots and tax evasion, which were historically the means by which people let their rulers know that they were pushing the limit of what was acceptable.

Another important feature of political history that follows on from its concern with the system of politics is that most political history is ultimately a history of political entities. That is, it is concerned with largely self-contained and self-governing communities and the political systems of those communities. This means that much of the political history of the world since 1800 is the history of national states. Some suppose that this is what political history always means. However, the case of the modern world is misleading in this respect. Political history is concerned with the history of political entities, which means primarily states and governments. (There is also the specialized topic of diplomatic history, which deals with relations between these entities.) Until very recently most states and governments have not been coterminous with nations and the attempt to make this so is the cause of serious anachronism. A history of the German nation in the Middle Ages would be primarily a cultural history and quite different from a political history of either the Holy Roman Empire or of one of its sub-units such as Bavaria. Political history, then, is the history not only of nation states, but also of all of those other kinds of polity that were once so common: empires, tribal states and confederacies, city republics, dynastic states and monarchies. Indeed, one of its functions now is to explain the workings of these kinds of political entity to an age that is largely ignorant about them.

Finally, as well as touching on the history of institutions, political history also overlaps with the history of ideas. This is because ideas and beliefs clearly play a hugely important role in politics. The concern here is not so much with the history of political thought. It is rather with the form that political ideas take in routine political debate and conversation, and the way these influence people's thinking and decisions. The focus is on the typical and intellectually average rather than great works of philosophy. It is the ideas found in political speeches, pamphlets and journalism that are of interest. The history of philosophy comes into play in so far as these ephemera are retailing the ideas of great thinkers second-hand.

► Political history – non-empirical and structural approaches

So political history is a complex topic, a study of the political process from a variety of angles. How, though, is it done, and what exactly has been the impact of empirical thought and method? Social historians, in particular, have been dismissive of political history, with J. R. Green's rejection of 'drums and trumpets' being repeated down to the present day. ('Kings and battles' has now replaced Green's formulation as the usual term of dismissal.) This view of political history as practised by professional historians is completely false. However, it is plausible because the older way of thinking about this subject, which still persists in popular historiography, did have some of that quality. The kind of work Green was disparaging is indeed little more than the higher form of gossip. Moreover, when writing political history, it is very easy to fall back into writing an unreflective account in which one thing simply succeeds another – just one damn thing after another as somebody once said. This kind of non-scholarly history has a number of forms, many of them longstanding.

One very old type, already alluded to, is the recounting in minute detail of the feuds, struggles, victories and defeats (and frequently love affairs) of the political elite and their hangers on. Some of this does indeed have the flavour of a gossip columnist. A famous example is the *Anecdota* or *Secret History* of the sixth-century author Procopius, with its venomous description of the court of Justinian and Theodora. The nineteenth and eighteenth centuries saw many such accounts, often in memoir form. Some of these are now important as **sources** because they give the views of a contemporary observer or participant in events, but they are not to be read as accurate history.

The dominant kind of political history in the Middle Ages, and for a long time thereafter, was an annalistic recounting of events that simply gave a chronological account with little or no effort at explanation. This is the kind of writing which does fit the description of 'kings and battles'. What is lacking in this is explanatory **narrative**, which not only puts events into order but also seeks to uncover the links and connections between them. A closely related type of writing is moralistic accounts. Here political events or the political career of an individual are presented with a view to drawing moral lessons. As churchmen were very fond of this kind of narrative, the lessons to be drawn were often of the perils of hubris and ambition and the great need to be generous to the Church. The opposite of this were narratives composed to explicitly flatter the powerful – Procopius appears to have composed the *Anecdota* while completing an official panegyric of this kind, which also survives. Once again this kind of literature is still with us, especially in 'official' (that is government sponsored) histories.

However, the most common alternative to an empirical approach to political history in modern times is one that treats politics and the political system as an **epiphenomenon** or consequence of something else. What this means, first, is that political history is seen as less fundamental or basic than the something else that determines it. The second result is that politics is by definition not seen as an autonomous activity. Consequently, political events are explained not in terms of the politics itself, but as the outcome of some other process. A specific example of this is the tendency to explain the outbreak of World War I as due to structural economic or social causes rather than the political decisions of the ruling elites of the time, particularly the German one.

There are many species in the genus of structural accounts of political history, but there are five that are cited most frequently. The most common today is the economic, which explains political processes, decisions and outcomes as the results of economic forces. (A slightly different approach is that of applying economic analysis to political action – this does not necessarily involve denying the autonomy of politics.) This kind of analysis is commonly associated with Marxism, but is actually just as common among economic liberals. Another, once common but now rare, sees all political (and social) life as the reflection of religious change, meaning alterations in the pattern of religious belief. Social organization or 'deep structure' is another recent favourite, particularly among authors from, or close to, the so-called *Annales* school of French historians. Here the argument is explicitly put that politics and political events belong to the '*histoire evementiale*', which is ultimately insignificant and no more than the foam on top of the sea of structural social history, to adapt Fernand Braudel's arresting image.[2] Social organization is also popular as a determinant of politics, although this tends to be linked to the economic model. One way of thinking was to see politics as being shaped and driven ultimately by a historical cycle of birth, flourishing and decay, which took place in all civilizations. This idea was very popular in the ancient world in the work of people such as Polybius and enjoyed a sudden resurgence in the twentieth century through authors such as Spengler, Toynbee, and Sorokin, but has now fallen out of fashion. Yet other ideas see political history as an epiphenomenon of genetics, race or geography.

All of these approaches to political history have certain common features. As well as making political history a subordinate element in the past, which cannot be explained on its own terms but only by reference to something else, they have two other consequences. The first is a tendency towards inevitability, a belief that there is only ever one possible outcome or class of outcomes to the political process in any given period. Applied to the present and prospects for the future, this can engender fatalism. When applied to the past, it leads to the conclusion that what actually happened had to happen, that there might have been a difference in detail but not in anything essential. In this way of thinking, because politics and political outcomes are ultimately determined by something else, political actors have very limited room for manoeuvre. If they have free will at all, they do so only within strict limits and so are constrained to act in a particular way. This means that the historian of politics (or of anything else for that matter) is reduced to demonstrating how the underlying forces, whatever they were, brought about the observed outcome. It also means that the role of the decisions and beliefs of individuals is downplayed, along with the impact of circumstance. This leads for example to the argument that Margaret Thatcher's being Prime Minister had little real effect on the politics of the 1980s – any Conservative leader would have put through much the same measures – or that German unification would still have happened, even if Bismarck had died in a shooting accident and never become Chancellor, because any leader in his position would have had to behave in much the same way.

The other possible consequence is to render most politics trivial, as the metaphor of Braudel cited above indicates. It means that the impact of political events on society and individuals is less important or profound than that of the other factor that is seen as more basic. In this way of thinking, the impact of the political process is ultimately ephemeral because it does not affect the 'structures of everyday life' (another of Braudel's phrases), unlike such forces as climate, economics or technology. The problem with this is that while some political events have little immediate impact on everyday life, others certainly do, most obviously war, the quintessential political act.

▶ Empirical political history

The empirical approach to political history rejects all of this. Anecdotal stories of faction fighting and annalistic narratives are to be rejected because they do not explain enough. **Structuralist** accounts are rejected for several reasons. Some are seen as overly deterministic. From an empirical point of view, it is clearly true that political actors move within a framework of institutions, expectations and social order that collectively limits their freedom of action. As said above, part of the historian's job in this view is to elucidate this framework and show exactly how it helped to determine the course of events. It is this that makes such works more than biography, whether individual or collective. However, there is no empirical evidence for the kind of elaborate determinist models alluded to earlier. For one thing such arguments fall foul of the **nominalism** of most empiricists. Entities such as classes or social groups do not declare war, engage in political struggle or seek power; these are shorthand ways of saying that individuals from these groups do these things. They may be representative, but that is not the same thing as saying that the category itself is an actor. There is also the problem of evidence. To say that a person acted in such a fashion, at such a time and for this or that reason is something that can be demonstrated by reference to sources. The existence of social forces is something that can only be inferred at best. Often it is assumed, in order to explain the recorded pattern of events.

A good example of this is the question of Henry VIII and the break with Rome in the 1530s. Obviously, this momentous event has attracted a lot of attention. The concrete details of the process, the dates of the various events, are not in dispute. The argument is over the explanation; why did this happen? Many explanations have been offered that would suggest that there was some inevitability, or at least high probability, as to the course that Henry took. The problem is that it is difficult to show the causal links in these structural explanations, which relate the Reformation to such factors as economic and social change, or a shift in class power. There is, however, plenty of evidence to support the straightforward explanation, that Henry took advantage of the arguments being produced by reformers when he was unable to get the annulment of his marriage that he desperately wanted for both personal and dynastic reasons.[3] The changes that the other explanations rely on may indeed have been happening. What is difficult is to demonstrate that there was a causal link between them and the events of high politics. Sometimes a connection of this kind can be shown, but often, on closer examination, it dissolves. The link is often made by simply asserting or assuming that politics is determined by some other factor, but when this is precisely the matter in dispute, such arguments have a circular quality.

The case of Henry VIII is also an illustration of another point – that while political actors are constrained to some degree they do have autonomy and can break or stretch those constraints, as well as having choice within them. The implication that these choices are trivial is simply false. There is something deeply ironic about Braudel formulating his description of political history as a surface event that did not affect the deeper currents, while he was in a POW camp as a result of a war that had the most profound effects yet was the result of political choices and events.

The rejection of these approaches also reflects the more general hostility of empirical historians to what they see as a theoretical approach. It would make more sense to see this as aversion to a particular kind of theoretical line or, more precisely, to a theoretical approach to the writing of history where the theory is ultimately what determines the pattern of research and interpretation, rather than empirical evidence. The outlines of an empirical political history are clear from the description already given. Obviously, it seeks to give at least an evidence-based account of events and the role of individuals in them. It looks at more than just events, however, as there is a concern with the 'rules of the game' as well. The principal aim though is to compose a particular kind of narrative, one that explains how choices, chances and structures interacted, and how one event or set of events led to or caused another. This involves weighing up the relative emphasis to give to different causal factors or events. One result is that because of the rejection of inevitability, narratives of this kind always involve implicit **counterfactuals**. That is, there is always an implicit argument that had something not happened the way it did, then other things would have happened differently. This process of counterfactual reasoning is not an analytical device, like the use of counterfactual models in **cliometric** economic history, but an essential element of historical judgement. If a historian of the English Reformation chooses to emphasize the importance of the king's dynastic concerns, there is an implicit counterfactual to the effect that had Henry and Catherine of Aragon's son lived, the break with Rome would probably not have happened. This is not the same as the kind of more elaborate counterfactual that is a frequent plot device in science fiction.[4]

Finally, as we saw earlier on in our discussion of Ranke, empiricism means a distrust of **teleology**, of the idea that history is moving towards some end state or goal. It also means, as we saw, that each time or period has to be treated on its own terms, not seen as simply a precursor to something else. This implies that no one period can be privileged, that there is no idea of certain times having an unusual significance or import. As we shall see, this has profound implications for much political historiography.

▶ Why political history is important for many empirical historians

The sources for political history are very diverse, in fact one could almost say that anything is grist to its mill. In practice research of this kind concentrates on certain specific kinds of record. Clearly, the political process itself generates records, such as the memoirs and correspondence of participants, political writings and polemic, and the records of political institutions. The context for all of this is provided by the records of administrative and other institutions and the kind of evidence drawn on by economic and social historians. The sources of cultural history can be used to discern the climate of opinion or zeitgeist.

This range of sources leads to another question. Why, in practice, is political history so central for many historians? The first answer, made forcefully by Sir Geoffrey Elton, is that this simply reflects the intrinsic importance of the subject itself. Political history deals with a fundamental or foundational aspect of human life, that is, the ways in which human beings live together in complex organized societies and conduct their affairs. This is fundamental because order is the basic social good: if humans are unable to make a political order work, the alternative is indeed a war of all against all, in which no other aspect of human social existence will be feasible. The study of the political process throughout history, in all its forms, is therefore of great importance. One point made by Elton was that political history, because of its methodological demands, is a more rigorous and precise discipline than political science, which he dismissed as 'present politics with newspapers'. As John Vincent has pointed out, we can know more about, and have a better understanding of, past politics as compared to present politics, both because there is more evidence to hand and because distance in time brings perspective.[5]

Granting, for the sake of argument, the importance of political history as such, why though should it have such great significance for historians of an empirical bent in particular? For the empirical historian history as an activity has two essential features. It is based on evidence and it goes beyond **antiquarianism** by seeking to explain causation through time, how one state of affairs became another. This necessarily involves constructing a narrative. Political history is the first choice of subject matter as the core of such a narrative. Political history in most cases has to be a narrative because it is the history of a process rather than a condition. There have been great works of analytical political history, such as Namier's *Structure of English Politics*, but these are important for historiography precisely because they have then been incorporated into the narrative. All of this is in contrast to other areas of historiography such as social history. Here the emphasis is on 'snapshot' studies that give an analytical portrayal of an aspect of society at one moment in time rather than on narrative. Elton illustrates this through analogy by likening political history to a river, studying the flow of lives and events through time, while, he says:

> It [social history] studies the static elements in the stream – the boulders, the jammed tree trunks, at best the eddies. Social analysis works by tactics which bring the stream to a halt, and it studies cross-sections ... But I draw your attention to the inadequacy of any historical analysis which is not predominantly directed towards an understanding of change through time ... A history simply is not equal to a collection or even a sequence of technically analysed sociological states.[6]

Moreover, as the range of sources given earlier indicates, political history is not only a topic that requires narrative. It is the topic that most readily lends itself to a narrative that can incorporate other topics and narratives. This may seem strange to students confronted by books that concern themselves only with the inner workings of high politics, but these are best seen as a special kind of political history rather than its template. A political history of twentieth-century Britain for example would have to incorporate economic, social and cultural history as well as the history of social policy, so as to have a political history that is comprehensive. The same would not be true of the other areas.

The persistence of empirical history is perhaps most marked in the area of political history. Here over the last 50–60 years there has been a strong challenge mounted, both to the empirical approach in general and to the conclusions of empirical scholarship with regard to certain questions. The last 20 years, however, have seen a reassertion of empirical methods and assumptions in this area. Many of the specific historiographical debates show two distinctive qualities. The first is the gradual but persistent move from a narrative that is teleological and has a strong element of inevitability to one that lacks both of these qualities, and emphasizes instead the contingent and the particular. The other is a movement away from large-scale explanations, and a focus on specific, carefully delineated questions to which research can yield definite answers. The reassertion of empiricism has also highlighted its principal problem, mentioned in the previous chapter, that is, the tendency of empirical research to ultimately undermine narrative and with it the capacity to understand change. The persistence of empirical political history, in the face of a challenge and an attempt to explore major questions of political history on a different basis can be seen in three well-known examples.

▶ Seventeenth-century England – the challenge to empiricism

The first challenge is the history of the British Kingdoms, and especially England, during the seventeenth century. That century, which saw civil war, the execution of one king and the replacement of another, has always been recognized as a momentous and significant one. Subsequent generations looked back and saw its middle decades as a kind of turning point, where their own political world had in some sense come into being. This means that the events of the seventeenth century in all parts of the British Isles have never lacked historians, nor has there been any shortage of debate, over what exactly happened, why it happened and with what result. The earliest were works by contemporaries such as Clarendon and Burnet. The title of Clarendon's work *The Great Rebellion* reveals in itself the perspective that he and many of his fellows brought to those events: they saw them as an eruption of disorder, a crisis of lawful authority. They did not, however, put them into any long perspective. Instead, they tended to stress the role of individuals, of Hampden, Pym, Charles I and James II, Montrose and Argyll.

However, the intellectual and political divisions that grew before and after 1688 and intensified after the Act of Succession meant that people came increasingly both to see the politics of their own time as deriving ultimately from the earlier convulsions, and to look for an explanation of those events that would justify their own position. This was true both for Tories and the several varieties of Whig, but it was the **Whigs**, as the party in power after 1715, who had most to gain from a history that would justify the outcome of their own position. Tories, by contrast, had a different need, to justify the system of which they were part but to do so in a way that enabled them to damn the Whigs. The eighteenth century saw several histories of the years between 1603 and 1715, all of which were in some degree or other partisan, inasmuch as they reflected the Whig or Tory 'take' on the events of those years. David Hume's *History of England* was explicitly written to undermine what he saw as a one-sided Whig narrative in the works of authors such as White-Kennet. The early nineteenth century saw Hallam's rejoinder to Hume. The Whig and Tory views of the Civil Wars, as we find them at the start of the nineteenth century, had their distinctive themes. The Whig view saw the events of 1640 to 1660 and later 1688 as the outcome of an attempt by the Stuart monarchs to subvert the established form of government. The Tory one, derived from Hume, stressed the part played by accident, the impact of religious enthusiasm, and the errors of Charles I and James II. Both saw the Revolution of 1688 as the triumph of common sense and compromise over fanaticism and obscurantism.

The later nineteenth century saw the transformation of the subject by empirical archival research. The towering figure in this process was S. R. Gardiner (1829–1902). His life work, the *History of England from the Accession of James I to the Outbreak of the Civil War*, along with its sequels, remains a landmark in the historiography of the period. What Gardiner did was to establish a factual narrative of the almost day-by-day progress of political events in early seventeenth-century England. This in itself was an enormous achievement. Revealingly, no one has questioned the basic **facts** as he set them out. Even the later historians who aimed to recast the history of the period in a non-empirical mould saw themselves as building on the work that Gardiner had done rather than replacing it.

Gardiner, though, did much more than provide an accurate **chronological** account. His narrative was also explanatory. The explanation he gave was the classic 'Whig' account in the historiographical sense of the term. The events of the Civil War, as he recounted them, were part of the progress of England towards Parliamentary government. The active role in the story was given to Puritanism, defined as a distinct religious and political movement within English protestantism which provided the leadership and the ideology of the parliamentary cause. One of the noteworthy features of Gardiner's work was the way it fitted into a series of works with the same general view, from A. F. Pollard's account of the early Tudors, via Neale's portrayal of the reign of Elizabeth and Wallace Notestein's description of the early Stuart period to his own work, and later that of G. M. Trevelyan on the reign of Queen Anne. It seemed there was a coherent narrative for English political history, from 1485 to 1715 at least. If Stubbs was added to the list, it went all the way back to 1066 and beyond. This was a series of narratives produced by the move to empirical research and methods, but shaped inevitably by contemporary concerns, and also very powerfully affected by the persistence of a teleological model of English history.[7]

What then happened was that from the 1940s onwards, there was a pronounced movement in the historiography in several new directions. The central element in all of these, traced by Alastair MacLachlan in *The Rise and Fall of Revolutionary England* was the attempt to redefine the events of the seventeenth century as a revolution, using the concepts and categories that had been applied to the French Revolution of 1789.[8] As MacLachlan points out, these categories had diverse roots owing much to nineteenth-century French classical liberalism and eighteenth-century Scottish sociology, but the immediate influences were Marxism and theoretical social science. So, as well as trying to recast the events as an abrupt break in history on the French model rather than as part of the upward moving historical escalator of English liberal progress, the new historiography sought to move away from a strict empiricism and to explain the past using theoretical models. The political history of seventeenth-century England was now to be explained using theoretical constructs such as the Marxist theory of stages of historical development and the theory of revolution developed by political scientists. It is important to realize that this did not involve a rejection of Gardiner's work *in toto*; it was the explanatory narrative that was being challenged rather than the factual detail.

This all led to a surge of publications. One aspect of this was a movement away from the traditional subject matter of high politics and a new interest in 'history from below', that is, the part played in political events by the common people. There was also an increasing interest in the ideas and role of radicals and dissidents from outside the mainstream of seventeenth-century politics. One of the first works in the new departure was a short book, *The English Revolution* (1949), by the young Christopher Hill. This gave a straightforward Marxist reading of the Civil War and Interregnum. They were the epiphenomenon of the development of capitalist relations of production, and the political upheavals were a class struggle in which the rising bourgeoisie were victorious. Hill went on to produce a stream of publications but moved away from the crude Marxism of his first book. Later, confronted with the difficulty of identifying the class divisions in the two sides of the Civil War, he argued only that the English Revolution had 'cleared the decks for capitalism'. Hill's retreat led him to concentrate more on popular politics and a culture of radical opposition to the established order. This was best expressed in his most successful book *The World Turned Upside Down* (1972). Meanwhile, other authors such as Brian Manning explored the part played in the conflicts by the common people, in works like *The English People and the English Revolution* (1976). Another fruitful move was the work of authors such as David Underdown, which explored the connections between cultural and religious attitudes and local economic organization, and traced the move towards deepening cultural and political splits in England in the decades before 1640. The use of models drawn from political science was most explicit in Lawrence Stone's *Origins of the English Revolution* (1972). This employed the political science theories of Chalmers Johnson, with elaborate distinctions drawn between 'preconditions', 'precipitants' and 'triggers' of revolution.

All of this involved both a widening of the scope of research and a change in the explanations given for the political events and outcomes. The narrative of Gardiner was replaced, even while the empirical evidence he had accumulated was used. It is important to realize, however, that more was involved. The role of a theory in Gardiner's account was implicit (and possibly unconscious), but in the historiography of the period from the 1950s to the 1980s it was explicit. Theory, whether derived from Marx, political science or a radical political tradition, was made to drive the analysis. Marxist scholarship suggested that if there was a revolutionary change in the political order, it was the result of conflict between an established economic and social order and the forces aligned with a newly emerging one. Social science models using an 'ideal type' of revolution produced the conclusion that catastrophic breakdowns in the political order were the product of a long-term loss of legitimacy followed by a short-term crisis or division within the elite. These explanations were assumed in the narrative and research was shaped by the need to find the examples and information that would reveal and flesh out what in principle was already known.

► Seventeenth-century England – the empirical response

The problem for the historians engaged in this enterprise was this. Motivated by theories of what revolutions were, they used these theories to explain the political history of seventeenth-century England by arguing that it had experienced a revolution of the kind described in the theoretical analysis. This was a serious attempt to generate a political history based on either a comprehensive theory of history and historical causation (Marxism) or the use of **ideal types**, rather than a strictly empirical programme. Research, however, constantly threw up information that did not conform to the models. Christopher Hill's work showed one response, to make the model more complex and less-clearly defined. This, however, meant that it lost much of its explanatory power and there was a danger that it would collapse into generalized platitudes of the 'people rebel when they feel a vital interest is threatened' variety.

The result was the appearance of what became known (inevitably) as revisionism. As one leading revisionist, J. C. D. Clark, has pointed out, this did not happen only in seventeenth-century studies. It also occurred in the historiography of the sixteenth, eighteenth and nineteenth centuries.[9] The common feature over all of these periods was a shift back to an empirical model of research and methodology. In the case of seventeenth-century English politics this had several aspects. The first was detailed local studies, starting with the work of Alan Everitt and John Morrill. These revealed a much less divided society than expected, with most members of the local elites trying to remain neutral. The second was the impact of detailed, not to say minute, study of the workings of early Stuart Parliaments. This was a result of the work of the History of Parliament Trust, set up in 1951 and for many years regarded as a wasted effort, accumulating no more than a series of lives of MPs. However, in the hands of Conrad Russell and Kevin Sharpe, this work radically undermined the idea of growing tension between Crown and Parliament in the period 1603–29. It became clear that there was no coherent opposition to the Crown and that all of the political actors shared common presumptions and language. More recently, Sharpe has reassessed the personal rule of Charles I and gone far in undermining the old idea of the 'eleven-years tyranny'. All this meant that the causes of the conflict, which had seemed so clear in Gardiner and so deep-seated in the historiography of 'Revolutionary England', became increasingly a matter of contingency. The third aspect of the renewed empiricism was detailed study of the process that had led to the outbreak of hostilities in 1642. The outstanding work here was Anthony Fletcher's *The Outbreak of the English Civil War* (1981), which traced in painstaking detail the breakdown of a general consensus in Parliament between 1640 and 1642, and the critical part played in this by the eruption of revolt in Ireland and the personal passions of Charles I and John Pym. Hill, meanwhile, had been the recipient of a devastating attack on his methodology by J. H. Hexter, which had a permanent impact on the reception of his work.[10]

All of this led to a new narrative of the political history of seventeenth-century England – or Britain, for one feature of revisionism was the incorporating of Scotland and Ireland into the story in a way that had not been true before. What appeared was a narrative that emphasized the short-term and contingent causes of conflict, the critical role of individuals, and the lack of deep-seated social or cultural divisions. This was the result of eschewing theory and concentrating on trying to answer smaller, more precise questions such as how Stuart Parliaments worked, how the Civil War had actually broken out in the localities, and exactly what sorts of people had played an active role on both sides. The result was much greater, more detailed knowledge and a more comprehensive narrative but also to dissolve the older teleological story, whether of the growth of liberty and representative government or the rise of capitalism. So, as in administrative history, there is a tendency for large-scale narratives to be replaced by localized, detailed and short-term ones, in which the cause and even direction of historical change becomes hard to discern. This provoked reactions not just from advocates of the notion of revolutionary England, but also from defenders of the older narrative such as J. H. Hexter.[11] One argument was that the new narrative produced by renewed empiricism was not actually atheoretical. The avoiding of explicit theory and concentration on small issues had only allowed an implicit theory to creep in and determine the outcome, one very similar to the argument made by Hume. Was this in fact a Tory history reborn? The critical difference was that the new revisionist narrative (unlike Hume's) no longer provided any justification of the political outcome of the events of the seventeenth century and seemed to mean that they had little real long-term significance. This disturbed many of the revisionists themselves. Another problem for them was to explain how a stable political order, marked by consensus instead of sharp divisions, had collapsed into a savage war that ended with the execution of the King. It seemed that empiricism did indeed dissolve all attempts at large-scale or long-term explanation.

▶ Eighteenth-century Britain

This same process and outcome can be seen in other examples. One where the outcome was perhaps less destructive to established explanations, but no less dramatic, was the political history of Britain in the eighteenth century. For many years this was the neglected era of British history, attracting much less attention than the seventeenth or nineteenth. An important influence was the adoption by historians of the generally hostile view of the eighteenth-century's politics and government taken by Victorian reformers. This made the eighteenth century no more than a backdrop to the process of modernizing reform. For a long time there was a fairly coherent picture of the politics and history of the period. The only significant innovation was the work of Sir Lewis Namier and his pupils, which showed that in the 1750s (and by extension, it was thought, the entire period after 1715) there were no real political parties but only shifting factions based on client–patron connections. Before 1715 was an age of sharp party divisions between Whigs and Tories. The defeat of 1715 effectively destroyed the Tory party in Parliament and ushered in 'pudding time', a period of political stability and quiescence where such divisions as did exist were between 'Court' and 'Country', little more than synonyms for 'in' and 'out'. The monarchy lost most of its power after 1715 with George I and II both disengaged rulers. Party divisions revived after the accession of George III and the age of political factionalism was definitively brought to an end by the crisis of 1782/3 which ushered in a new age of party with a (second) Tory party confronting the Whigs. In wider society the eighteenth century was marked by the early stirrings of the industrial revolution, which had undermined a stable landed society by the end of the century.

Almost none of this has survived recent research. Linda Colley and Eveline Cruikshanks discovered that the Tory party survived until the 1750s (now seen as somewhat aberrant) and that the division between Whig and Tory remained sharp. The work of Ragnhild Hatton restored the first two Hanoverian monarchs to centre stage. Detailed study of the electoral history revealed a larger electorate and a more active politics than the nineteenth-century stereotype of elections in Eatanswill. The economic history of authors such as Nicholas Crafts replaced the industrial revolution by a story of much slower and more localized economic change. Jonathan Clark put together a synthesis of the new findings in 1985 in *English Society, 1688–1832*, in which he argued that to understand society in that time you had to see it as it was: a stable, hierarchical *ancien régime* confessional state, not different in kind from any other regime of the time, even France.[12] The eighteenth century also could not be seen in teleological terms as the progenitor of liberal democracy and industrialism in the subsequent century.

► The French Revolution (?)

While empirical political history was wreaking havoc among long-term theoretical historiography on one side of the Channel, something similar was happening on the other. The French Revolution did not suffer the fate of the English Revolution – a historical term now commonly discarded. That there had been a revolution of some kind after 1789 was undoubted. That it marked a great division in history was also the view of almost all historians, from the romantic republican Michelet to the hostile conservative Taine. Interestingly, one of the few to argue that while catastrophic it had been essentially a chapter of accidents was its earliest historian, Archibald Alison (1792–1867). In the central years of the twentieth century the historiography of the French Revolution had two principal models to hand to use as the basis for a narrative. The minority tradition was the 'Atlantic Revolution' of R. R. Palmer and Jacques Godechot, which saw the events in France as part of a wider movement towards democracy and modernity that included America and the Austrian Netherlands. The more influential view was the one associated above all with Georges Lefèbvre and A. Soboul which saw the collapse of the *ancien régime* after 1789 as the outcome of a process of social change in eighteenth-century France, the central feature of which was a bourgeoisie growing steadily wealthier, more influential and more resentful of its exclusion from office.[13]

The assault on these structural explanations began as early as 1954 with an attack by Alfred Cobban. The real problem, however, was that once again detailed local research using empirical methods produced findings that did not fit either of the models. In 1967 G. V. Taylor published a seminal article in the *American Historical Review* arguing that the empirical evidence simply was not there for the model of a rising bourgeoisie or nascent capitalism. He went on to make use of an underused source, the *cahiers de doléances* (lists of grievances) handed into the Estates General in 1789, and argued that these did not demonstrate any clear desire for radical reform or the influence of subversive ideas. Subsequent research tended to confirm Taylor's arguments and the idea of the Revolution as the outcome of long-term social and political development began to dissolve, just as it had in England. This again led to a focus on the short term, particularly the crises and on the actual political process, now seen as the cause of radicalism rather than its consequence. This emphasis on the Revolution as a catastrophic breakdown in the political order found expression in the very influential works of François Furet while other historians such as Lynn Hunt explored the part played by language and rhetoric in changing the perceptions of the historical actors.[14]

The outcome again was a more complex, contingent picture and narrative with the idea of a structural explanation for events discarded. What was left in all of these cases was an empirical narrative that traced how one event led to and produced another without any overarching explanation or **metanarrative**. The idea of a sharp divide in the past, of a sudden move from one epoch to another, which was embodied in the theoretical idea of a Revolution was progressively eroded away, even in France, just as Fustel de Coulanges had undermined the idea of an abrupt end to Roman civilization in Gaul and economic historians were to cast doubt on one of their central notions, that of an industrial revolution. This all meant that no period or event could claim particular significance in the course of history. In this respect the revisionist historians of the later twentieth century were reverting to the position put long before by Ranke. As Alastair MacLachlan puts it:

> In a famous aside Ranke enjoined historians to accept the relativity of their enterprise: there were no privileged ages, no chosen races, not even special classes – each epoch was 'immediate to God'. For the first time, perhaps, a genera-tion of seventeenth-century scholars arose who took him at his word and who were not out to demonstrate that their period was of overwhelming and demonstrable importance in the creation of the modern world.[15]

It was not only in the area of seventeenth-century scholarship that this took place. In political history of every period the empirical turn after about 1970 reasserted the model of scholarship that Ranke had articulated and applied it more strictly than ever. The result was to show both the power of that model and its problems.

6 Economic History and Empiricism

▶ The nature and origins of economic history

Economic history has interesting and complicated origins. From one perspective it arose from the application of orthodox empirical method to the study of economic matters, previously reserved for a select species of **antiquarian**. Another view would have it that the critical event was the introduction and application of economic **theory** and method to these antiquarian studies. The first view emphasizes the paternity of history, the second that of economics. Both imply that economic history, while part of the historical family of disciplines, has a relationship with economics, which can give it an exotic or hybrid quality.

A rather different view of the origins of economic history as a subject comes from students of the history of economic thought. Here economic history arises from a bitter struggle within the discipline of economics over its methodology and definition towards the end of the nineteenth century. The side that ultimately lost the argument then branched off to become the subdiscipline of economic history. This can be read as implying that a kind of intellectual divorce took place between history and economics around the start of the twentieth century. Certainly, the subsequent history of economics lends support to this view, with a move into ever higher levels of mathematical abstraction since 1945, but not all economists agree with this or think it a good thing. Joseph Schumpeter, for example, argued that historical study and analysis was an essential part of the economist's work and actually rated it higher than the other two elements he identified, statistics and 'theory'.[1]

In the discussions over the location of economic history, three questions are put. How does economic history relate to the other two disciplines – is it history which concerns itself with economic matters or a kind of economics that is based on history? What is the relative importance in the work of economic historians of economic theory and empirical historical research? How important is historical perspective for economists, and economic thought for the study of history?

The reality is that empirical enquiry and economic analysis have both played an important part in the study of economic history over the last 120 years or so. For a long time empiricism undoubtedly had the dominant role and one of the functions of economic history has been to puncture the certainties of theory. To begin with, the two disciplines of economics and history are inextricably interconnected. Modern economic thinking initially grows out of a largely historical analysis. Later, there is a separation, although there is argument about the date, with some locating it in the 1820s, others the 1880s. As we shall see, I would argue that the case for the 1880s is the stronger. At the time of the separation between mainstream economics and economic history, the latter becomes increasingly an organized profession with an empirical method, in the same way as conventional history, with Germany once again leading the way.

The scholars who have pursued this largely empirical research have been trying to answer a fairly limited number of specific questions about the economic aspects of the past. Economic history has been dominated above all by one big question with many ramifications, that of how and why a 'modern' economy came about in the later eighteenth and early nineteenth centuries. Interestingly, this can be seen as the modern form of the intellectual problem that brought about the emergence of economics in the first place.

As D. C. Coleman remarks in his survey of economic history in Britain:

> The origins of economic history as a subject of study in Britain are to be found in eighteenth-century Scotland. The writings of the Scottish Enlightenment, and more specifically of the Scottish historical school, provided the first British signpost to the examination of the economic past as an essential element in the understanding of human society.[2]

The same period saw similar intellectual developments elsewhere, most notably in France with the writings of the Physiocrats such as Quesnay and Turgot. At this point in intellectual history the two disciplines of history and economics were not fully formed and the genres of economic and historical writing were not distinct. Many of the leading figures in the speculative literary histories of the **Enlightenment** such as William Robertson were also important for the ancestry of economics. In fact, we can go further. In its origins, economics, or political economy as it was then called, had a kind of historical analysis as one of its central elements. Speculative history as to the origins of civilization, wealth and commerce was one of its intellectual driving forces. The great question for eighteenth-century authors was the one that economists have made their own – what is wealth, where does it come from and what are its effects? The attempt to answer this led authors such as Adam Smith to explore the past as well as the present.

One starting point for such explorations was the interest in the beneficial effects of trade and commerce from the 1690s onwards. This found expression in the literary works of a series of authors from Defoe and Addison onwards. A repeated theme was the 'softening' or 'polishing' effect of commerce and wealth as they replaced crude, barbarous manners with refined ones. This was typically articulated through a historical account of the movement from barbarism to civilization, with commerce given the central part. An important example of this was the long *Introductory Essay* to Robertson's *History of the Reign of Charles V*. However, in this, and in authors such as Hume and Kames, the historical detail was subordinated to a discussion of morals and manners. Above all there was no real attempt to use concrete historical examples or empirical **fact** (other than the actual recent history of Scotland): the history was highly speculative.

It was with Adam Smith that a theory of history and historical development, derived in part from authors such as Robertson, became central. Although the *Wealth of Nations* is best known now for its discussion of such matters as the division of labour and the case against mercantilist trade policy, a large part of it (most of Books III and V) is concerned with an elaborate **stadial** model of history, designed to explain how the commercial society of Smith's own time had grown out of the feudal society and economy of the Middle Ages. In his great work (and even more in the earlier *Lectures on Jurisprudence*) Smith combines theories of human nature and society with empirical evidence drawn from **antiquarians** and the history of antiquity. As Coleman points out, the two elements do not always combine easily. The works of Smith's contemporaries Adam Ferguson and James Millar also feature this combination, particularly the latter's *An Historical View of the English Government* (1787).

▶ Early economic history in France and England

A common view is that this development of an historically aware economics was suddenly cut short from the 1820s by the sudden eruption of abstract, ahistorical reasoning in economics. The blame for this is put on militant utilitarians such as James Mill, but above all on David Ricardo. According to this account, historical reasoning of the kind found in Smith was abruptly cast out of economics for several decades. Consequently, authors such as Coleman and Harte argue, history and economics went their separate ways for some 50 years, with economics becoming an ahistorical, theory-driven discipline and history concentrating on matters political and constitutional while ignoring economic affairs. Coleman does allow that classical economists such as McCulloch used historical illustrations in their argument but, as he says, this was not the same as actual history-based analysis.[3] Instead, historical snippets mined from antiquarian scholars were used as weapons in contemporary debate. At the same time historians such as Hallam and Macaulay chose to concentrate on constitutional history and ignored the economic history of such authors as Millar as being too speculative. As Hallam tartly put it:

the work of Professor Millar of Glasgow, however pleasing from its liberal spirit, displays a fault too common among the philosophers of his country, that of theorizing upon an imperfect **induction**, and very often upon a total misapprehension of particular facts.[4]

It would be hard to find a clearer instance of an empiricist dismissal of economic theory when applied to history.

In fact, the apparent divorce of history and economics was never so clear-cut. It is true that political economy took a sharp turn towards abstraction and theory and away from the concrete and empirical with the publication of Ricardo's *Principles of Political Economy and Taxation* in 1817. It is also true that most historical writing in Britain during the period 1820 to 1860 was concerned with **narrative** political and constitutional history. This reflected the difficulty of doing any other kind of research before the appearance of an organized historical profession – Macaulay remarked that the famous 'third chapter' of his *History of England* (on social and economic conditions) had been as difficult to write as the rest of the work put together.

However, as Coleman admits, there was a good deal of empirical study of the historical aspect of economic matters going on during those years. Most of it was not scholarly, but then neither was most of the mainstream history being written. In the first place there was a continuing tradition of economic antiquarianism. The best known example of this, Adam Anderson's *Historical and Chronological Deduction of the Origins of Commerce* (1764), was brought out in a completely revised version in David Macpherson's *Annals of Commerce* in 1805. Macpherson also produced a *History of European Trade With India* in 1812. This kind of writing continued long after 1820, one very popular work being the *History of British Commerce and of the Economic Progress of the British Nation, 1763–1870* (1870) by Leone Levi. There were also many studies of the history of particular industries and localities. At the same time the tradition of speculative history with an economic aspect survived for some time, one important work being *On the Rise, Progress, and Present State of Public Opinion* (1828) by William McKinnon.

However, the most significant feature of the mid-nineteenth century was the continuing development of economic history as an academic subject. This tends to be overlooked for a number of reasons. One is that initially it took place outside Britain, in France and Germany. Another is that a crucial part was played by methodological disputes between economists, which have been studied only by historians of economic thought. The main reason, however, is the retrospective definition of their intellectual ancestry by the two disciplines of history and economics. After both were consolidated as academic disciplines at the end of the nineteenth century, there was a process of constructing an intellectual ancestry or pedigree. Many authors were cut out of this family tree for one reason or another.

This was particularly the case in economics because of the part played in the evolution of the discipline by the methodological dispute alluded to earlier. As a result, a whole range of empirical and historically minded thinkers have been largely deleted from the standard genealogy because they do not fit into a line of descent from Ricardo via J. S. Mill to Jevons, Menger, Walras and Marshall.

In Britain the historical aspect of political economy found in Smith did decline in prestige with the ascendancy of Ricardo. (It continued in economic populariza-tion as well as in the works of authors such as Richard Jones (1790–1855), but that, as they say, is another story.) In France and Germany things were very different. In France Smithian ideas persisted, in the works of J. B. Say and his followers. Two of the most important of these were Charles Comte (1782–1837) and Charles Dunoyer (1786–1862). An elaborate stadial theory of history and historical development was at the centre of their thinking. This came from the five-stage model found in Smith, but was more elaborate and extended Smith's outline into a sophisticated argument which related most aspects of life and politics to the economic organization of society in different periods of history. They also worked out an influential model of class division, dividing societies between the 'industrious' or 'working' classes who produced wealth, and parasitic groups who obtained it through force. This again was given a historical evolutionary basis.[5]

These ideas were an essential element of the arguments of the so-called 'French liberal' school of political economy. They also had a marked impact on the thinking of nineteenth-century French historians who incorporated these economic argu-ments into their histories. One very important example of this was the *History of Civilisation in Europe* (1846) by Guizot. A more direct influence can be seen in the work of Augustin Thierry, particularly his *Origin and Progress of the Third Estate* (1859). The historical writings of the 'French school' and of those historians influenced by them were initially in the mode of Enlightenment speculative history but the empirical element grew steadily. They began by using the work of eco-nomically minded antiquarians for illustrative purposes, but increasingly carried out direct empirical research themselves. The result from the 1840s onwards was a number of important (and large!) works of empirical economic and social history by authors such as P. E. Levasseur (1828–1911), Jerome-Adolphe Blanqui (1798–1854) and Charles Gide (1847–1932).[6]

▶ **Economic history and historical economics in Germany**

The rise of economic history in Germany was even more central for both history and economics. Economic history, or at the very least history concerned with economic matters, was an important part of German historiography from the very start, with works such as the *Reflections Concerning the Politics, Intercourse, and Commerce of the Leading Nations of Antiquity* by A. H. L. Heeren, one of the leading lights at the eighteenth-century University of Gottingen. In France a form of political economy which was historically minded generated historical inquiry. In Germany it was the historical investigation which came first and then produced economic arguments, even if this was done under the spur of the ideas of British classical economics. The key figure was Wilhelm Roscher (1817–1894). Other important writers were Bruno Hildebrand (1812–78) and Karl Knies (1821–1898). In 1843 Roscher published *Outline of Political Economy According to the Historical Method*. This was both a work of economic history and a manifesto for a particular approach to the study of economic matters, one that was empirical, inductive and historical, as opposed to the theoretical, **deductive** and abstract approach of the British classical school. Part of his argument was a programme of research and this was followed up in works such as Hildebrand's *Economics of the Present and the Future* (1848) which looked at such matters as the history of trade, agricultural organization, wages and the use of money.[7]

These early German economic historians, like their counterparts in France, were still very much influenced by the abstract system building of the tradition of speculative history. The idea of stages of historical development was especially persistent. By the 1870s, although these ideas could still be found, as for example in the works of Karl Bucher (1847–1930), the practice had come to focus on detailed empirical study of historical case studies or of specific economic phenomena. This was very much the case in the works of the man generally seen as the head of the German 'historical school', Gustav von Schmoller (1838–1917). The historical school argued that to pass from axioms via abstract reasoning to general economic principles was to do things the wrong way round. For them the validity of general economic laws was conditional on the specific historical context. So, for example, concepts such as market prices and supply and demand, while appropriate for understanding the nineteenth century, might be useless in the study of the Middle Ages. Schmoller went so far as to deny that there were any 'laws' in economics. This made empirical historical research the main activity for the economist.

In the early 1880s an intense, often very bitter argument erupted among economists over the nature and content of their discipline. The '*Methodenstreit*' as it was called in Germany, raged like a forest fire for several years. The other side of the argument to the German and French **historicists** were the new mathematical economists such as Leon Walras, William Stanley Jevons and Alfred Marshall. They all advocated what became known as the 'marginalist revolution' in economics, one aspect of which was the application of the integral and differential calculus to the analysis of economic processes. It was this movement, with its emphasis on the timeless, ahistorical concept of equilibrium, that definitely made economics a primarily ahistorical and theoretical discipline.

▶ The formation of empirical economic history in Britain

For it was the mathematical marginalists who were to win the argument in Britain and Germany, and even in France. In Britain, while there had not been a recognized 'historical school' of economics as in France and Germany, there were a number of important figures who had argued for an empirical and historical approach. The two most important ones, Thomas Cliffe Leslie (1825–1882) and J. K. Ingram (1823–1907) were both associated with Trinity College, Dublin. (Ingram was actually the professor of Greek there.) In 1875 Cliffe Leslie made the case for the German historicist approach in an article in the *Fortnightly Review*. In his other writings he used empirical argument and example to criticize the deductive approach of the Ricardians.[8] The main problem at this time for historians and economists who wished to explore the economic past through empirical research was the difficulty of finding enough accessible data. Too much of the economic **sources** were scattered and uncollected. This was because much of it, not being directly related to government affairs, was not in public archives. One person who made an important contribution to redressing this, and to the formation of economic history generally, was James E. Thorold Rogers (1823–1890). Between 1866 and 1902 he brought out the eight massive volumes of the *History of Agriculture and Prices in England* which collated, organized and analysed a huge mass of information about the historical levels of prices and wages. His other works, such as *The Economic Interpretation of History* (1888) and *Six Centuries of Work and Wages* (1889) were the first real examples of empirical economic history in Britain, particularly the latter. Amongst other things, Rogers was able to demonstrate the broad outlines of the historical levels of real wages, emphasizing the sharp rise in the fourteenth and fifteenth centuries and their decline in the sixteenth.

As Cliffe Leslie's article showed, there were also people in Britain who were influenced by the German historical school in particular and took its part in the local front of the *Methodenstreit*. The two main ones were William Cunningham (1849–1919) and W. J. Ashley (1860–1927). Cunningham, in particular, had a long-running series of disputes with his Cambridge colleague Marshall, over the syllabus, the nature of economics, and the relations between economic history and economics. As Ashley remarked later (in 1893 and again in 1900), the outcome was that, having failed to convert the general body of economists to their way of thinking, they settled down on their own fenced-off academic territory, as economic historians.[9] Ashley himself became the first person in the world to hold a chair of economic history, as opposed to economics, when he moved to Harvard in 1892.

Between about 1885 and 1925 economic history became an institutionalized academic profession. Key events were the setting up of the London School of Economics in 1895 (it became part of the University of London in 1910), the creation of the first full-time paid lectureships in the subject in 1904, 1905 and 1907 at LSE, Manchester and Oxford, and the creation of the first chairs in the subject in 1910 and 1921. Its professional organization, the Economic History Society, was set up in 1926 and its own '**learned journal**', the *Economic History Review* in 1927. As with mainstream history, Britain lagged some way behind Germany, where the subject-specific 'learned journal' had been started in 1903.[10]

Cunningham and Ashley had brought out two of the early examples of scholarly, empirical economic history during the 1880s, that is, Ashley's *Introduction to English Economic History and Theory* (1888/93) and Cunningham's *Growth of English Industry and Commerce* (1882). Both of these were critical not only of the intellectual approach of the economic mainstream, but also of one of its central policy prescriptions, that of free trade. This critical view of economic theory and its impact on policy was also found in another significant work from that decade, the posthumously published *Lectures on the Industrial Revolution in England* (1884) by Arnold Toynbee (1852–1883). This was important for two reasons. First, because it invented the concept which was to dominate economic history not only in Britain, but in other countries as well. Second, because it was an important part of the other principal source of economic history in Britain besides the historical school of economic thought. This was the growing interest in the later nineteenth century in what was known as 'the social problem', which found expression in works of investigation such as Seebohm Rowntree's *Poverty: A Study of Town Life* (1901) and Charles Booth's *Life and Labour of the People in London* (1889–1903).

▶ The early years of professional economic history

The rise of an empirical economic history followed the same pattern as the one traced in Chapter 2 for history in general. Originally there were both antiquarian studies and speculative historical narratives, concerned with economic matters. These gradually combine to produce scholarly empirical economic history. The additional element is the role of economic categories and definitions, which create what one economist has called the 'economic point of view'. This has given economic history a distinctive quality apart from its subject matter. As Cunningham put it: 'Economic history is not so much the study of a special class of facts as the study of all the facts of a nation's history from a special point of view.'[11] The appearance of a scholarly practice was consolidated by the institutionalization of a profession with all the apparatus of journals, chairs and academic careers.

The pattern of historiography which emerges in economic history is like the one we have already discussed in the history of institutions. In the beginning there is a narrative based on research, but often owing much to **myth** and not empirically based. A problem of interpretation is identified or a question is formulated. This leads to document- and record-based research. This in turn casts doubt on aspects of the original narrative, which has to be amended. It also throws up new questions and opens up new topics of research. Over time the questions become more narrowly focused and come to deal with finer points of detail.

Since the later nineteenth century economic history has focused on a number of specific questions, but one topic above all has been dominant. This is the whole set of questions associated with the Industrial Revolution. By the end of the nineteenth century all commentators had become aware of just how different their own society was from all other historical communities. This found expression in J. M. Keynes's remark that George Washington had more in common with a Roman centurion than someone born two generations later, so great had been the changes of the nineteenth century. It was clear that the central change was economic, a total transformation, it would seem, of the economic organization and conditions of life. This gave the newly emerged discipline of economic history a clear agenda: to uncover what exactly had changed in economic life between about 1750 and 1850, why this change had happened, and with what effects. There were always other areas of interest, but even these tended to be defined by their relationship to the big, central question. Thus, the study of economic affairs in the ancient or medieval world was mainly about learning more about the way things had been before industrialization, in the 'lost world'. The underlying question driving studies of the economic history of the world outside Europe and North America was that of why these places had not (yet) experienced a transformation like that of Europe.

The history of economic growth in Britain and the pivotal change of the later eighteenth century were the subject of a number of early works. Cunningham's *magnum opus*, which went back as far as the Middle Ages, has already been mentioned. After Toynbee, the writers who had the greatest influence were the husband and wife partnership of J. L. and Barbara Hammond. They were not themselves professional academics, but rather amateur scholars of the same sort as the Webbs and the Bosanquets. The Hammonds produced many books, but their great work was the trilogy of *The Village Labourer* (1911), *The Town Labourer* (1917) and *The Skilled Labourer* (1919). These were polemical works, portraying the years 1750–1850 as marked by the appearance of class divisions and the ruthless use of political power by the rich in their own interest. For them, the economic changes of the period may ultimately have benefited society in general, but for several generations redounded solely to the profit of the wealthy, while the poor were dispossessed. The Hammonds's impact was considerable and their picture of the process of industrialization still dominates the popular mind. Their work was entirely unquantified and made no use of economic models. The same was true of other early works such as Ephraim Lipson's *Economic History of England* (1915–30).[12]

The person who introduced quantitative argument based on empirical evidence to this topic was J. H. Clapham. His *An Economic History of Great Britain* (1926–38) is one of those works usually described as 'monumental'. Certainly it was an amazing achievement for its time and was reissued as late as 1964. Clapham relied mainly on printed **primary sources** such as Blue Books and government commissions of enquiry. He also made extensive use of the information contained in local and national antiquarian works, along with memoirs. In general he did not use such records as company papers or manuscript ones such as Poor Law records, partly because these were still not readily available. He was able to draw on the increasing number of monographs, most of them studies of specific regions or industries. Clapham's work therefore was a synthesis of the existing knowledge, as it stood in the 1920s. While he adopted a rigorously quantitative method, he did not make use of the models of economic theory which he had already criticized elsewhere as 'empty boxes' (in the modern vernacular we would speak of a 'black box').[13] His work was therefore highly empirical.

▶ Empirical debate – standard of living and quality of life

What Clapham did do was to draw a coherent picture of the growth of an industrial society in Britain, one that severely amended the dark portrayal of this process by the Hammonds. This in turn led to much more research and generated a number of specific debates, some of them still continuing. These demonstrate both the empirical nature of the arguments on both sides and the way that knowledge of a whole range of topics has progressed since the 1920s, to the point where Clapham's great work is now of interest mainly to the historiographer.

The best known of these debates was that between 'optimists' and 'pessimists' over the standard of living of the majority of the population between about 1770 and 1850. The pessimists, following on from the Hammonds, argued that there had been a decline in the standard of living of the working classes up to 1850. (No one denied that there had been a rise in the standard of living after that date.) The optimists, starting with Clapham, argued that at the very least things were not as bad as they had been painted. Increasingly, they argued that there had been an actual rise in the standard of living of the majority. These were of course empirical quantitative questions and could only be given an answer by establishing such matters as the level of wages and prices on a firm footing. This could only be done by very painstaking research, none of which was easy. This was one reason why the debate went on from the 1920s to the 1970s. By the early 1960s this kind of work had produced sufficiently firm figures to broadly vindicate the 'optimists' so far as the real level of wages was concerned. Some authors such as Eric Hobsbawm kept up the good fight, but by the 1980s a much clearer picture had appeared. This was that real incomes were stable over the country as a whole between 1750 and 1790 (although there was a rise in the North and Midlands, and a decline in London and the South). The years 1790 to 1815 saw stagnation or decline, associated with the effects of the Napoleonic Wars. However, the evidence for the period between 1815 and 1850 is clear-cut: there was a substantial rise in real wage rates and by 1850 the average working man earned 72 per cent more than in 1810 or 53 per cent more than in 1819. This went along with much more exact knowledge of variations between regions and different categories of worker.[14]

This led to a shift in the argument, which amounted to a new debate over what became known as 'quality of life'. This had two aspects. One was an argument about relative, as opposed to absolute incomes. Might it be the case that although workers real wages had risen in absolute terms, the gap between them and the wealthier classes had grown so that they were worse off in relative terms? The second was over non-monetary aspects of the standard of living. The question here was whether or not the bulk of the population, while enjoying a rise in real wages, had not experienced a decline in such matters as the quality of their diet, the attractiveness of their environment, and the amount of free time at their disposal.

These are even more difficult to answer than questions about wage and price levels because of the great difficulty of quantifying some of them, or of finding adequate data. Moreover, they could not even have been meaningfully explored on an empirical basis until the first questions had been broadly answered. The tactic adopted has been to look at indicators for which there is evidence, such as height (an indicator of diet), mortality rates (particularly infant mortality), and income and wealth distribution as revealed by sources such as income tax returns and probates. Here the debate is still continuing, but already the main conclusions are emerging. These are that quality of life, as measured by such factors as height and life expectancy, did not improve dramatically between 1815 and 1850 in the way that wages did, but showed no decline either. For inequality, it would seem that there was a growth in inequality of both income and wealth in the same period, and possibly before, followed by a dramatic decline in both income and wealth inequality in the twentieth century.[15]

▶ The debate over enclosures

Another debate which came out of Clapham's disagreements with the Hammonds related to the nature of agricultural change during the 1750–1850 period and, above all, to the role of enclosures. In the view of the Hammonds these had impoverished the smaller farmers and agricultural workers, and had driven large numbers of people off the land and into the new, industrial towns and cities. This view had already been challenged by R. E. Prothero in *English Farming Past and Present* (1912). He emphasized the way that agricultural output had grown during the eighteenth and nineteenth centuries so that Britain could feed a rapidly growing population. The Hammonds had not denied this, but had emphasized the social cost of the form this 'agricultural revolution' had taken.

Research into this question made use of such sources as the papers and maps associated with enclosure acts, the estate papers of major landlords, and the records of agricultural prices and wages. The most important work to come out of these was J. D. Chambers and G. E. Mingay's *The Agricultural Revolution, 1750–1880* in 1966. As well as doing research themselves, Chambers and Mingay made use of many small-scale empirical studies of enclosure that had been done since the 1950s. Their conclusion was that there had been a revolution in agriculture in the eighteenth century, that enclosures had played a key part in this, and that, on balance, they had benefited not only the landlords but also the small farmers. Other research, by authors such as Eric Kerridge, put forward a different **hypothesis**, that the real breakthrough in agriculture had taken place in the sixteenth and seventeenth centuries. Historians following up on this hypothesis have tended to argue that the improvement in productivity was not connected to either enclosure or the growth in the size of farms.

The Hammonds have not recovered from their mauling by Chambers and Mingay. However, a new generation of historians has now subjected Chambers and Mingay to criticism in their turn. They accept their empirical findings and support the idea that a large increase in agricultural productivity was essential if Britain was to avoid a Malthusian crisis. However, they argue that the benefits did accrue mainly to the landlords by showing that most of the smallholders whose title was recognized in the enclosures were bought out soon afterwards. The focus now is on evidence for a rise in labour productivity and on the impact of institutional change, especially in property rights.[16]

Meanwhile, the research mentioned earlier has led some historians to revive one of the Hammonds's arguments, that enclosure and a diminution in the number of farmers was not necessary for the rise in agricultural output. Comparative research on the economic history of the Continent, and particularly France, indicates that it was possible to retain a much larger proportion of the labour force in agriculture in a modernizing economy than was the case in Britain. Comparative studies of economic change in different countries have become a growth area in their own right in recent years. Initially, the central question was that of why industrialization had happened first in Britain rather than France, and the argument of most works was that historians had to explain why this process was delayed in other parts of Europe such as France and Germany. The key work was that of Alexander Gerschenkron, particularly his *Economic Backwardness in Historical Perspective* (1968). Again, research has tended to amend the initial thesis and more recent works on the pattern of industrialization in Europe are as much a matter of several different routes or types as they are of 'retardation'.

▶ Other empirical debates

Since the 1920s a number of other issues have arisen around this broad topic of economic growth and development in the modern world. These include such matters as technological change, the history of business organization, the nature and sources of wealth in Britain over the last 200 years, and the rate of economic growth over the same period but particularly during the years 1750 to 1850. The great figure in the history of business organization is Alfred D. Chandler, particularly through the trilogy *Strategy and Structure* (1962), *The Visible Hand* (1977) and *Scale and Scope* (1989). These built on the appearance of analytical (as opposed to antiquarian) business histories, such as the history of *Unilever* (1954) by Charles Wilson. They have in turn generated many detailed studies which, in the usual way, are now leading to a reassessment of Chandler's model. The debate over wealth and its origins is at an earlier stage, partly because historians have until recently spent more time studying the poor and the working classes than the rich and middle classes. Unexamined presumptions in this area have been upset by the work of W. D. Rubinstein, most prominently in *Wealth and Inequality in Britain* (1986). By using evidence from probates he has been able to show that throughout the eighteenth and nineteenth centuries, the very rich in Britain gained most of their wealth and income from the traditional sources of land, trade and finance rather than manufacturing. In fact, large manufacturing fortunes were comparatively rare.

The most vociferous debate in recent years has been over the rate of economic growth during the early phase of British industrialization. At one time economic historians were unable to attach meaningful quantities to notions of economic growth during this period. However, the detailed research done in the central decades of the twentieth century made it possible to address this question. In 1962 Phyllis Deane and W. A. Cole brought out what was for many years the definitive work on the subject, *British Economic Growth 1688–1959: Trends and Structures*. They argued that the evidence showed a relatively rapid rate of growth. However, later work, particularly that by Nicholas Crafts and C. K. Harley, indicated that the actual rate, while not insignificant, was less than Deane and Cole had thought. The problem was that they had taken much of their evidence from precisely those parts of the economy that were experiencing the most rapid growth.[17]

In fact, the conclusions arrived at by many economic historians during the 1980s led them to downplay the scale and rapidity of change during the years 1750–1850. Eventually, some argued that there had never been an industrial revolution in the way the term had been understood since Toynbee. This was apparently an instance of research not only qualifying the original model but dissolving it entirely! However, this view has not won general acceptance and has attracted strong rejoinders from R. M. Hartwell, and Maxine Berg and Pat Hudson. Something happened, seems to be the common view, even if it was less dramatic than once thought.[18]

▶ Empirical research and the growth of knowledge

The reality is that some 80 years after the arguments around the history of industrialization began, we now have much greater knowledge than was the case in the 1920s. The extent of this growth of knowledge can be seen by comparing Clapham's three volumes from the 1920s and 1930s with its contemporary counterpart *The Economic History of Britain Since 1700*, edited by Roderick Floud and Deirdre McCloskey. It is revealing that the later work is a compendium of articles by many hands; no one person could now do what Clapham could in earlier years. In this area of economic history, as in political or institutional history, we can now make more definite truth statements about a wider range of topics and these can be made with a greater degree of precision.

This advance, as in other areas, has been arrived at primarily by empirical research rather than the perfection of theory. On the other hand, economic theory has played a part. Economic principles and concepts have been used essentially as **heuristic** tools. They have acted as guides to research and have generated expectations as to what research is likely to uncover, and also what the likely explanations of findings would be. So the classical theory of trade and the concept of opportunity cost (that is, that the true measure of the cost of any choice is the value of the foregone second choice) have played this role in the study of, amongst other things, the part played by trade in economic growth. However, theory has played a subordinate role to empirical research. You do not find authors arguing 'such and such a finding cannot be true because it would violate an economic law' or 'theory predicts that X will be the case, therefore we already know what we will find'. It is knowledge based on evidence that trumps theory. Moreover, the theories of economics when used by historians have been employed to generate testable hypotheses, which can then be checked against the information derived from the sources.

Naturally, although the study of industrial society and its origins has been the primary interest of economic historians (not least because the records are more abundant), other areas have also attracted interest. One pioneer was the Belgian Henri Pirenne, who had the rare distinction of having a historiographical thesis named after him. Rather like Clapham, he set in train a whole set of interrelated debates, in this case about trade in the early medieval period, the origins of medieval towns, and the nature of the 'Dark Age' economy, which continues to this day. In Britain the most influential economic historian of pre-industrial England for many years was R. H. Tawney (1880–1962). Like the Hammonds, he stimulated much debate, through works like *The Agrarian Problem in the Sixteenth Century* and *Religion and the Rise of Capitalism*, but has had most of his detailed argument discredited by later research.[19]

▶ The empirical history of slavery and 'cliometrics'

One specific topic in economic history that has attracted much attention is that of colonial slavery and the transatlantic slave trade. Until 1944 the history of these topics was dominated by a moral narrative of hostility to slavery and veneration for the campaign against it by figures such as Wilberforce. That year saw the publication of Eric Williams's *Capitalism and Slavery*. This introduced economic thinking and analysis and put forward a number of specific hypotheses, that slavery had generated an important part of the capital used in the early phases of industrialization; that the slave trade had brought many important institutions and trade infrastructure into existence; and that slavery and the slave trade had been abolished not because of a moral campaign, but because they were less and less profitable. These were all supported by empirical assertions on Williams's part and were empirical, testable claims. The consequence of his pathbreaking work has been a succession of detailed empirical studies of the economics of slavery and the slave trade. Perhaps the most important for further study was Philip D. Curtin's *The Atlantic Slave Trade: A Census* (1969) which, by using commercial records, was able to give firm figures for the total number of slaves sent across the Atlantic. Later works, particularly those by David Eltis, Roger Anstey and Seymour Drescher, undermine or even disprove important aspects of Williams's argument and also call into doubt assumptions of economic theory such as the inherent economic inefficiency of slave labour. For example, Drescher argues in *Econocide: British Slavery in the Era of Abolition* (1977) that the slave economy in the West Indies was more profitable than ever at the time of abolition. Anstey argues that while the slave trade was indeed highly profitable, it was too small a part of the overall British economy to have been responsible for any substantial amount of investment. In recent years our knowledge of the working of slavery as an economic system has developed considerably due to quantitative economic history, starting with the (very controversial) work by William Fogel and Stanley Engerman *Time on the Cross* (1974). The current trend is for wider comparative study of slavery in different societies and eras and of unfree labour more generally.[20]

Fogel's work is important for more than just slavery, for he was perhaps the leading figure in the renewed input of economic models and theory into economic history that took place after the 1960s. This phenomenon is usually known by the term **'cliometrics'**. This expression includes two related but distinct phenomena. The first is the use of sophisticated mathematical and particularly statistical analysis of the data of economic history, often employing the categories of post-Keynesian economics such as national income. The second is the use of economic models, usually taken from neoclassical economic thought. Fogel's first major foray into this kind of work was *Railroads and American Economic Growth* (1964), where he used these techniques to work out how different the American economy would have been had the railway not existed and, by doing this, establish how much railways had contributed to economic growth in America (the answer – not very much). This kind of argument has played a major part in recent work on British economic history, as can be seen by scanning the three volumes of Floud and McCloskey. Not all of the response has been welcoming. Geoffrey Elton had doubts, expressed in his exchange with Fogel in *Which Road to the Past*. As said above, however, the use of statistical analysis and economic concepts and categories does not in itself challenge the empirical underpinnings of economic history. It could rather be seen as giving them greater rigour. There is more doubt about the use of models and it was this aspect of Fogel's own work that attracted the most criticism.[21]

▶ The future of empirical economic history

The area where economic history is perhaps most likely to grow is comparative and global history. From its origins one of the questions that exercised economic historians was, as one article put it, 'Why is the whole world not developed?', or in other words, why did a modern economy first appear in Europe? In the 1960s and 1970s this attracted even more attention, due to the contemporary concern with questions of economic development. In the early 1970s some outline explanations were put forward by E. L. Jones, D. C. North and R. P. Thomas. These drew on North's own work in economics, which emphasized the role of institutions, such as property rights, in economic processes.[22]

At about the same time a quite different explanation for the economic history of the last 500 years was put forward by Immanuel Wallerstein in his multi-part work *The Modern World System* (1974/80). Simultaneously, Fernand Braudel brought out a massive structural analysis of global economic history, *Capitalism and Material Civilisation* (1979). A series of schematic works have now been written on the subject of global comparative economic history, of which the most successful has been David Landes's *The Wealth and Poverty of Nations* (1998). None of these is empirical in any meaningful sense. We are now in the early stage of the inductive cycle, with the appearance of local empirical studies and works that break new ground such as Janet Abu-Lughod's *Before European Hegemony* (1989).[23] These are leading to questioning of the synoptic surveys of books such as Landes's work and will doubtless lead to a new, empirically based, synthesis in the second stage of the research cycle.

Today, economic history is still recognizable as a sub-discipline of mainstream history. Economic historians are often more self-conscious about the empirical nature of their work than the historical profession in general. This reflects the history of their sub-discipline and its origins in part in the *Methodenstreit*, and also the regular contrast between their own work and the more abstract endeavours of economists. Today, the relation between theory and, empiricism may be about to undergo another shift. There are signs that economics is retreating from the mathematical obsession that possessed it during the 1970s and 1980s. As a result economists are once again interested in empirical research, including history. A slightly different process, which has already had an impact on other academic disciplines, may now be touching history. This is the phenomenon of 'economics imperialism' in which economic analysis and reasoning is applied to areas not usually thought of as within the domain of economics. The best-known cases are the work of Gary Becker on such topics as marriage, suicide and the family, and Richard Posner on the law and criminality. This has been going on for some 30 years in areas such as sociology and politics. It may now affect history, through such moves as the application of public choice theory to political history and modern micro-economics to social history. If this does happen, it would be simply a reassertion of Cunningham's maxim, that all aspects of the past can be studied from the economic point of view. However that may turn out, it seems certain that no matter how sophisticated the analysis, it will have to do its work on the knowledge gained by rooting around in archives: if it fails that test, it will be rejected.

7 History of Ideas – The Empirical Turn?

▶ A Trojan Horse?

Intellectual history, or history of ideas, is the most problematic area of history from the empirical point of view. This is because it is difficult to combine empirical methods and the history of ideas by virtue of the very nature of the topic. Moreover, the practice of the history of ideas inevitably raises the kind of issues that lie at the heart of the **postmodernist** critique of conventional history. History of ideas, like economic history, partly originates as an aspect of another discipline, in this case philosophy. Not surprisingly, most history of ideas has been in reality the history of philosophy, particularly political philosophy. However, in more recent times it has seen a widening of its subject area with a movement towards the history of common ideas and concepts. This is one aspect of the methodological revolution that has overtaken intellectual history in the last 30 years or so. A more long-standing but related process is the study of culture which, while a distinct area of **historiography**, is very closely related to intellectual history.

The starting point must be the question: 'In what sense, if any, do ideas have a history?' It is (apparently) clear what we mean when we speak of topics such as the history of a state, an institution or economic life. In such cases we are referring to the story that can be told of the origins and fortunes of the subject through time, as revealed by the **sources** it has generated. In what sense, though, can this be said of an idea? There are several possible answers. One is to argue that ideas as such cannot have a history because they are in a very real sense timeless. According to this view, what is thought of as history of ideas is actually a specialized form of philosophy or literary criticism. Another response is that while we can talk meaningfully about the history of ideas, such a history cannot by its very nature be an empirical history in the way that (for example) political or economic history can be. A third answer would be that given a correct method, an empirical history of ideas is possible but also that such an exercise will be strictly limited in what it can achieve. This means that much of what passes for history of ideas does not fall into the category of empirical history but is something else.

A final view that some historians may well hold, even if they do not admit it, is that history of ideas is a topic best avoided. In this way of thinking, intellectual history is the Trojan Horse that brings the subversive ideas of postmodernism and philosophical **idealism** within the citadel of empirical history. One problem is that ideas derived from literary criticism and philosophy, through their employment in the history of ideas, gain purchase in mainstream historical writing. This view is plausible at first sight. The reality is that certain ideas and methods taken from literary criticism can be very useful in the practice of the history of ideas. A case in point is **hermeneutics**. Hermeneutics is the systematic study and analysis of texts in order to discover what meanings can reasonably be ascribed to them in addition to the obvious, apparent meaning (if any), and to reconcile clashes of meaning in works by the same author or in the one work. It originated in the study of Biblical and legal texts. In the case of the Bible the aim was to apply the scriptural text to the present by discovering meanings in it that were not explicit when it was first revealed. This might involve replacing earlier readings of the passage. Another purpose was to reconcile apparently conflicting passages within the Bible. This was also the case in legal scholarship, as in the case of canon law where medieval lawyers sought to reconcile discordant (that is, incompatible) canons. The techniques of hermeneutics can be very useful to historians of ideas, particularly in discovering how the understanding of the meaning of a text came to change through time.

However, the uses made of hermeneutics by historians on the one hand and literary critics or philosophers on the other are two quite different things. The critic seeks to discover *new* meanings in the text while the historian is interested in recovering the *original* meaning and the *subsequent* understanding of the text. They are trying to achieve very different things, even if they use the same tools. The postmodernist rejoinder is twofold. First, that the distinction drawn here does not exist and the historian's activity is the same as that of the critic, because the past readings of a text are fundamentally unrecoverable (and may not even exist in any meaningful sense). Second, postmodernists go further and argue that *all* historical research and writing is a hermeneutic exercise in creating new meaning rather than recovering past meaning. It is with respect to intellectual history that such ideas are most plausible.

Why this should be so is clear. The claim of empirical history is that the events and persons of the past had a real, physical existence that we can no longer directly perceive, but which we can indirectly reconstruct from the traces they have left, that is, from sources. The postmodernist argument is that in this area, as in others, we can understand and reason only through the use of words, which have an almost unlimited plasticity of meaning. Consequently, what happens is not a recovery of the past by a type of detective process, but a kind of discussion through which words from the past and about the past acquire a meaning, that meaning being determined by the circumstances of the discussants. With people or events, only the most bold would deny that they had a real physical existence, even if it is now irrecoverable because of the limitations of language. This is not so with ideas. In what sense does an idea such as 'liberalism' or 'sovereignty' have a physical existence? Ideas of this kind exist, it is argued, only as words. The word *is* the idea, there is no 'thing' to which the word refers. Moreover, nobody denies that words do indeed change and shift in their commonly understood meanings. This makes ideas as entities highly plastic and in a way, ahistorical. Perhaps they at least can only be studied using literary analysis?

Well, no actually, is the response of many historians. Many or even most ideas do have some kind of physical **referent**, even abstract concepts such as 'sovereignty'. The referent is typically some concrete practice or institution that embodies the idea in the view of most people familiar with it at a given time. Moreover, complex ideas or systems of ideas (for example 'liberalism') have a complex structure and it is this that the historian seeks to capture. The practitioner of the history of ideas has two broad aims, one modest, the other rather more ambitious. The more modest one is to discover what words and modes of argument meant in the past, how they were used and what they referred to, and how these changed over time. The aim is not to uncover a timeless, eternal meaning, nor to discover a new meaning that might be useful for contemporary debates. Above all, it is not to find present ideas in the past. Rather, in Rankean fashion, it is to find out what the understood meaning of ideas was at a given point and how that state of affairs had come to be. The more ambitious goal is to recover, through this kind of study, the contents and structures of the minds and thoughts of people in the past, both as individuals and in the mass, as they were reflected in language and forms of expression. This is usually known by its French name, as '*Histoire de mentalités*'.

▶ The origins of intellectual history

Given this, how though should it be done, and can it be done in a way that fits in with the empirical practice dominant elsewhere in history? The answer from the historiography would appear to be that it is possible, but that much written under the rubric of intellectual history is not empirically based. History of ideas is both old and new. Old, because the very roots of history as a way of looking at the past are to be found in the efforts of early modern jurists to reconstruct a body of ideas in its original form (Roman law). New, because the last 30 years have seen an upheaval in the methodology of the history of ideas, the effect of which has been to put much of the work now done in this area on a more firmly empirical basis.

As with other forms of history, history of ideas first appeared as a scholarly activity in the middle to later nineteenth century. Looking at early works in this area, it becomes apparent that the intellectual impetus for this kind of work had three initial sources. The first was the appearance or explicit definition in the early nineteenth century of the main political ideologies of the modern world, liberalism, conservatism and socialism. From the 1850s onwards, exponents of these ideologies (mainly philosophers) sought to construct an intellectual history or genealogy for their beliefs, which involved studying the expressed ideas of people in the past and appropriating them as founders or originators of the system of belief they espoused. For various reasons, liberals were more active in this regard than either conservatives or socialists, at least initially.

The second factor encouraging an interest in this area was the growth from the mid-nineteenth century onwards of organized Freethought, that is **scepticism** about the claims of revealed religion, especially Christianity. As an intellectual movement Freethought had been around since the early eighteenth century but had been confined to a small section of the elite. (It was also dangerous to propagate such views because of the threat of prosecutions for blasphemy.) It became more prominent and widely expressed from the 1840s onwards. One of the main intellectual efforts of freethinkers was to trace the historical evolution of ideas, both Christian doctrine and sceptical ideas, which they saw as forerunners of their own beliefs. Naturally enough, this also provoked a response from believers.

A third impetus for intellectual history was the tradition of cultural history that developed by the mid-nineteenth century, of which the best-known example is the *Civilisation of the Renaissance in Italy* (1860) by the Swiss historian Jacob Burckhardt (1818–1897). This involved the study of the ideas and beliefs of people in the past as they found expression in art, literature and customary ways of life. This was made the basis for a programme of historical research by the German historian Karl Lamprecht (1856–1915).[1] He argued that historians had to abandon their, as he saw it, narrow focus upon political and institutional history. Instead, they should try to practice *Kulturgeschichte*. This meant the history of culture in the widest sense, including ideas, beliefs and mental feelings. This became linked in Germany with the **historicist** ideas of Dilthey (see above, pp 39–40). The idea was to study the culture of the past so as to empathize with it and come to understand its viewpoint.

Looking at the historiography of intellectual history up to about the 1930s shows three broad categories of writing, defined by their central subject matter. (Of course, these overlapped and some works can be placed in more than one category, but as a rule of thumb this is accurate.) The first were histories of Freethought, **science** and **rationalism** in general. The historical evolution of ethical ideas and beliefs was a prominent feature of many of these. Among the many examples of this kind of work were the voluminous writings of J. M. Robertson, an important figure in the disciplines of sociology and economics as well as history of ideas. Two of his best-known works in this were the *History of Freethought in the Nineteenth Century* (1929) and the *Short History of Freethought* (1915). Another author of this sort was the Anglo-Irish historian W. E. H. Lecky. He was a significant political historian and the author of a large work on the history of eighteenth-century Britain, but his work in intellectual history has stood the test of time better. *History* *of European Morals from Augustus to Charlemagne* (1869) was a history of ethical ideas which drew a contrast between the notions of the ancient world and those associated with the rise of Christianity. *The Rise and Influence of Rationalism in Europe* (1865) traced the growth and development of scepticism and scientific ideas at the expense of religion. Histories of science, or more properly of scientific thought, have been produced by many authors since Lecky's time.

The second kind of works were studies of political thought and ideas, or of abstract concepts. One famous example of this was *The Idea of Progress: An Inquiry into its Origin and Growth* (1920) by J. B. Bury. Many works tried to trace the appearance and development of modern political ideas, particularly liberal or socialist ones. The English socialist thinker Harold Laski was one noted exponent of this, in works such as *English Political Thought From Locke to Bentham* (1920) and *The Rise of European Liberalism* (1936). Another was G. P. Gooch, in *English Democratic Ideas in the Seventeenth Century* (1898). Again, works of this kind continued to be produced for many years.

Cultural history of the kind produced by Burckhardt and Lamprecht was more common in Germany than other parts of Europe. Elsewhere its greatest success came in the United States, where this kind of history was a central feature of the so-called 'New History' advocated by figures such as James Harvey Robinson (1863–1936) and his pupil Carl Becker. Cultural history of this kind frequently took the form of histories of 'civilization' or of the cultural 'legacy' of past times. Such works clearly harked back to the speculative histories and histories of manners that had been such a prominent feature of **Enlightenment** thought.[2]

▶ The nature of traditional intellectual history

All of these kinds of intellectual history shared certain common features. They used the same kind of source material and employed it in much the same way, and their arguments and analyses tended to follow a common pattern. The sources used were in general the canonical texts or great works of intellectual tradition, as defined by later scholars. Thus, histories of political ideas concentrated on writers such as Hobbes, Locke, Bentham and J. S. Mill, histories of economic thought looked at Adam Smith, Ricardo, Malthus, Mill and Marshall, while cultural histories concentrated on the great artists and authors such as Raphael, Dante, Petrarch and Rembrandt. In histories of science there was a similar canonical list of figures such as Galileo, Newton and Darwin. The main sources used were thus the original works themselves, not so much the less well known ones from the same date or the **secondary** works that responded to them or drew upon them. The only real exceptions were the cultural histories, which employed evidence as to the intellectual habits of everyday life such as correspondence, journals and newspapers and other ephemera.

Many of the works produced in intellectual history in the late nineteenth and early twentieth centuries are still in print or have been until recently, something that is not true of other areas of historiography. This should tell us that it was an area of study that saw relatively little progress in terms of greater knowledge or certainty. Looking at such works reveals several kinds of argument, none of which survived in other areas of historiography but had much greater longevity in this one. One kind of analysis that occurs repeatedly is the attempt to trace how a particular idea or way of thinking (such as rationalism or liberty) was 'discovered' or 'unfolded'. The underlying assumption was that in some sense the idea had always existed, but had not been fully understood or articulated and the historian's task was to show how, gradually, the understanding of the idea had grown. Another metaphor that shapes much of this historiography is that of refinement, where the idea or set of ideas is refined and better defined over time, with inconsistencies gradually identified and removed. The study of individual authors, such as Locke, concentrates upon the part they played in this process. This way of thinking makes ideas themselves timeless and eternal: it is only their manifestation in writing, art and argument that is historical.

One result of this approach is a kind of '**whig history** of ideas', in which there is a progress from lower, incomplete realizations of an idea to a higher, more complete expression. This means that the same kind of idea or argument can be cast as 'progressive' at one time, but as 'reactionary' at a later date. It also leads to the idea that people can be 'ahead of their time' in terms of their beliefs, as though there were a timetable for intellectual progress. This kind of argument is most common in the history of scientific thought and of disciplines such as economics, which see themselves as scientific, but it is frequently found in the history of political thought as well.

Another common feature of much history of ideas is the related, but distinct notion of an 'essentialist' approach to the study of ideas as found in writings and other forms of expression. Here literary techniques are used to extract the core essence of a past person's ideas and beliefs, as found in their writings. The elements in their work that are clearly the product of specific historical circumstances are discarded or ignored. The aim is to identify the ahistorical, Platonic essence of the idea, which can then be examined using the techniques of philosophical analysis. Where the study is concerned with a wider period of time and more than one person, the aim is to look at the form that an idea, such as liberty for example, has taken in the writings of various authors for purposes of comparison. The great problem with this approach is a tendency to **anachronism**. Emphasizing the common elements of the ideas of people widely separated in time and place can result in their being made to seem much more alike than they actually were. The individual who until recently suffered as much from this as anyone was John Locke, seen as a kind of liberal but with important parts of his thinking, such as his unorthodox religious beliefs, ignored. This also results in attempts to find a coherence in the ideas of an individual author that may well not exist. Just as theologians employed hermeneutics to reconcile the contradictory messages of the various parts of scripture, so commentators on Marx, for example, would try to uncover the common meaning of his earlier and later writings. The idea that his ideas might have changed over time was not examined.

A third common type of analysis was a kind of genealogy of ideas. This was especially frequent in the history of political thought. Here ideas are seen as being handed down through a succession of thinkers who extend and elaborate them, rather in the way that a house can pass down through a family with each generation making alterations and enlargements. There is a distinct element of truth in this, particularly when the individuals concerned see themselves as belonging to an intellectual 'family' and consciously draw upon the writings and arguments of the figures they identify as their 'ancestors', but this again takes ideas out of their full historical context and makes them partly timeless, this time as a kind of heirloom passed down over the generations. It is also much more difficult to demonstrate this kind of intellectual descent than one might imagine, very often it is simply assumed rather than demonstrated.

The final repeated feature is analysis based on the idea that ideas are simply the intellectual expression or rationalization of material circumstances. Here changes in expressed belief over time or the ideas expressed by people in the past are seen as the outcome or product of some factor such as geography, economics, class relations or the repeated patterns of everyday life. This kind of approach, found for example in the two works by Laski mentioned earlier, is most often associated with Marxism, where ideas are part of the **'superstructure'** the nature of which is ultimately determined by the 'base' (meaning the way production is organized). However, there are non-Marxist versions of this as well.

What all of these approaches reveal is the influence on much history of ideas of other disciplines and their concerns, particularly the disciplines of political science and philosophy. Both of these are concerned with ideas in the abstract, as timeless and unlocated. (In political science this is not always true, but is so in those cases where ahistorical categories such as Weberian **'ideal types'** form the basis of the argument.) There is also a marked interest in the concerns of the present, with ideas that are seen to be ancestral to present-day thinking receiving attention while others are ignored. As a result ideas and categories that have meaning for the modern world are applied anachronistically to the past. This partly reflects the origins of much history of ideas in nineteenth-century political and religious argument. At the back of all this, however, is a non-empirical way of thinking, which includes figures such as Kant and Hegel but ultimately goes back to Plato. In this, the ultimate reality is a timeless state that we do not directly perceive. Ideas and essences ('ideal forms' in Plato's terminology) exist in this ultimate reality. We observe the form these take in actual historical time and space. What is not prominent in much history of ideas until recently is the strict or thorough application of empirical methods as spelt out by professional historians from Ranke onwards. However, there has been a distinct move in this direction.

▶ A. O. Lovejoy and the notion of 'unit ideas'

The person who made the greatest contribution to intellectual history before the 1960s was the American philosopher A. O. Lovejoy (1873–1962). He was not himself a historian, but a philosopher with an interest in the history of the ideas he studied. In his own writings on **epistemology** he espoused a mixed kind of argument that combined empiricism and idealism. He is principally remembered, however, as a historian of ideas. His central innovation, which he began to formulate as early as 1905, was the notion of the 'unit idea'. He defined this (inasmuch as he ever did) in his best-known work *The Great Chain of Being* (1936). He started by arguing that history of ideas was not the same as intellectual history in general, which he defined in much the same way as Lamprecht. History of ideas for Lovejoy had five main elements.[3]

The first of these was the study of 'unit ideas'. These were 'persistent dynamic factors, the ideas that produce effects in the history of thought'. They bore the same relation to complex ideas or systems of thought as atoms to molecules. History of ideas was, for Lovejoy, not interested in large complex intellectual constructs such as 'God' nor in systems of thought such as 'isms'. These were both secondary phenomena that could be explained by reference to unit ideas. Unit ideas were of four broad types: unconscious assumptions or mental habits, which were not spelled out but had to be inferred; particular methods or ways of reasoning, such as nominalism; 'susceptibility to metaphysical pathos', that is, the association of ideas or words with feelings that they evoked; and philosophical semantics, that is, the generally understood meaning at a given time of particular words.

The other four elements of the history of ideas for Lovejoy all depend upon the concept of the unit idea. First, unit ideas are identified and traced through all of the areas of intellectual activity where they could be found, so literature, philosophy, art and culture generally are all part of the raw material for tracing their effect and impact. Second, this is done without regard to national or linguistic boundaries. Third, the historian has to look at the manifestations of the unit ideas in large groups of people, in their observable patterns of speech and behaviour. Finally, history of ideas looks at how new unit ideas arise, that is, at the process of intellectual change.

Lovejoy's arguments had a great impact on the historiography of ideas from the 1930s onwards. This impact was amplified by the part he played in the emergence of history of ideas as a distinct sub-discipline. Thus, in 1940 he founded the *Journal of the History of Ideas* as the '**learned journal**' for this topic. His own position as a philosopher engaged in history, and the implication of his own theories meant that under his influence, history of ideas became markedly interdisciplinary, even more than it had been before. In general, Lovejoy's approach led to a much greater emphasis on the detailed historicity of ideas, as entities that were located in time by virtue of having a definite time of origin and (sometimes) demise. This also meant more concern with the context or particular expressions or uses of unit ideas in order to explain how it came to have that effect at that time and place. The subject matter of the historiography became both more varied and more abstract, due to the interest in foundational unit ideas such as 'class' rather than complex ideological systems. One effect of this was that the analysis of the ideas became rather more rigorous and came to draw on a more varied kind of source material, due to the insistence on exploring the impact of unit ideas in all areas of intellectual life.[4]

However, his ideas also attracted much criticism. The principal difficulty for many was the nature of his key concept itself, the unit idea. It was not clear in Lovejoy's own writing exactly what counted as a unit idea and he never formulated a method for identifying them or rejecting candidates for that status. The notion of indivisible intellectual atoms that were the foundation of more complex ideas struck many as inherently implausible. As with the analogous case of elementary particles in physics, it was not clear where the process of division could, or should, stop. Also, while his method led to a focus on the historical use of unit ideas, they themselves did appear to be timeless, inasmuch as while the use made of them might vary, the unit ideas themselves remained unchanging. Above all, this is a kind of historical reasoning that is **theory** driven and rests on an *a priori* method (that is, one where a fact or statement is assumed and its consequences and ramifications then explored). The vital first step in this approach is to identify and define the unit ideas to be studied. This is done essentially through analytical philosophy. The first appearance and subsequent vicissitudes of the idea are then explored using historical methods. However, because the content of the unit idea is defined at the start, this determines exactly what will be looked for and found in the records. It is fair to say that Lovejoy's own work was free from many of the flaws identified by his critics. He tended to see the compounds formed by combining unit ideas as unstable and so emphasized the fluidity of ideas in practice, and he did pay more attention to the intellectual and social contexts of expressed ideas than his own theory predicted.

▶ The empirical revolution in history of ideas

It was in the 1960s that a major breakthrough took place in the methodology of history of ideas. Known (inevitably!) as the 'new intellectual history', it was associated with four scholars linked by their connection with Cambridge University. These were Peter Laslett, John Dunn, J. G. A. Pocock and Quentin Skinner. They shared a common interest in the history of political thought, in particular the political thought of seventeenth-century England. They shared a concern with the way that the political thought of this period was generally presented at this time (the 1950s). They were critical of both the 'whiggish' approach of authors such as Gooch, which emphasized transhistorical continuities and anachronistically cast figures such as Locke and the Levellers as liberals, and of the Marxist one that saw political thought as the determined outcome of social structures.[5]

These Cambridge scholars argued instead for a less present-minded and more empirical approach. This meant a focus on the actual sources for ideas, that is, the texts in which they were expressed. It meant an emphasis on the context in which those texts had been produced, both social and intellectual. In other words, the sources for history of ideas had to be treated in the same way as any other kind of source, and analysed in the same way rather than treating them as timeless messages. Of central importance in understanding them was the question of the audience for which ideas and arguments had been produced and the debate or conversation of which they were a part. One of the early triumphs for this approach came in 1960, with Laslett's edition of John Locke's *Two Treatises of Government*. This work had been originally published in 1689, immediately after the Glorious Revolution of 1688. It was assumed that the work had been written at that time, as an apologia for the *coup* that had overthrown James II. This led later scholars to see Locke as an apologist for the new regime and the advocate of a moderate, rationalist whiggery that would later become liberalism. Laslett was able to show that the *Treatises* had in fact been written in 1679–81, at the height of the Exclusion Crisis, at the behest of Locke's patron, Lord Shaftesbury. It was therefore a defence of rebellion, written at a time of political crisis and before any upheaval had happened. Laslett was also able to show that the *Two Treatises* were a response to the arguments of the Tory thinker Sir Robert Filmer. All this completely transformed the view that historians took of Locke and his ideas (see below, p. 121).[6]

However, the attempt to create a more rigorous method for the history of ideas still faced the philosophical problem of defining what it was that anyone could know about past ideas, and how exactly this could be discovered. It was Quentin Skinner in particular who addressed this question. From 1969 onwards he published several articles which tried to establish a sound method.[7] This worked in the following way. We cannot know anything about past ideas that have not been expressed in a form that has physically survived, directly or indirectly. Therefore, history of ideas is the study of the expression of ideas – these are the traces or remains that have been left by ideas that existed in the minds of people in the past. Skinner argues that history of ideas has to avoid two faulty methodologies. The first, popular with philosophers, is to look only at the text itself and to ignore the historical detail of its author and time of origin. This leads to several kinds of anachronism, which Skinner surveys. The second is to concentrate solely on the context and see the ideas as somehow necessarily produced by that context. The problem here is that the pattern of cause and effect only goes one way, from context to text. In reality the text itself and the act of producing it also have an effect and help to shape the context.

So, history of ideas involves the study of both texts and context. What connects them is a theory of the nature of communication, which Skinner got from the English philosopher A. L. Austin. In this way of thinking **'speech acts'** or **'utterances'**, which include such things as speaking, writing, publishing and performing, are actions which take place within a set of agreed rules that define their meanings as understood by the authors and audience. A speech act such as a written text has two kinds of meaning. The first, the **'locutionary meaning'**, is defined by the commonly accepted meaning of the words employed and can be discerned using the techniques of philology. The second, the **'illocutionary meaning'**, is produced by the purpose or intent of the author and gives the speech act its 'force' or 'point'. For example, a book written today might argue that control of money is a defining feature of sovereign power. The locutionary meaning can be discovered by exploring key terms such as sovereignty. The illocutionary meaning requires knowledge of the context in which the argument was made. So, knowing that it was produced in the 1990s as part of a debate over the European single currency is necessary in order to grasp the full point or purpose of the text as it was understood by its recipients. So, full understanding of the sources used in the history of ideas requires attention to both text and context.[8]

Skinner argues further that discovering the full meaning of the historical sources and thereby tracing the history of the ideas they articulate requires four steps. First of all, the historian has to reconstruct the background or context of the speech act, this includes such matters as the political, institutional and social background. Second, they have to explore the literary context into which the speech act fits. This is done by looking at other texts from the same period that examine the same subject matter. One very important aspect of this is to look at typical or average works rather than the great works that are remembered now, many years later. This is because the great works are, almost by definition, not typical of their time or of the debates of which they were a part. It is because they challenged conventional assumptions and ways of arguing that they are now seen as significant by philosophers. The third step is to discover what kind of vocabulary was available to the author of the speech act. This means not just the words available to them, but the expressions and systematic ideas and concepts that they could draw upon and employ to make an argument. The final step is to look at the way intellectual change happened, by examining historical arguments and seeing how these led to shifts in the meaning or understanding of key terms as well as the development of new ones. The ultimate aim is to reconstruct the meaning and organization of ideas and their expression in the past and the way these changed, without falling into the trap of present mindedness – all very Rankean.[9]

As well as Skinner's work, Pocock also contributed to the argument through the notion of '**discourse**' – a term that has a rather different meaning in his work to the one it has in postmodernist writing. He argues that at any point in time, participants in intellectual or political argument are not free to say anything that they like except in a trivial sense. The reality is that they have to employ a 'discourse', that is, a vocabulary of terms, arguments and figures of speech that exists at the time they contribute to the continuing discussion. These organize and limit people's understanding of, and response to, events. In particular they define what can be said and how it is said at a given time. If the vocabulary is not suitable or available, certain ideas and responses to events will become difficult or even impossible to articulate. On the other hand, the process of discussion can gradually alter the content of the vocabulary by shifting the understood meaning of key terms and introducing new ones. The historian, using the kind of methodology described, has to identify the elements of such vocabularies, and trace the way they shape responses to events and are amended by them.[10]

▶ The impact of empiricism on history of ideas

The result of the new method in practice was a series of works, mostly in the history of political thought, which overthrew much of the work of the earlier generation of historians. John Dunn, building on the work of Laslett, brought about a radical change in the perception of Locke and his ideas. Instead of being seen as a moderate, rationalist, proto-liberal, he is now understood to be a religious and Aristotelian thinker, backward-looking in many of his ideas, but also a radical, even a revolutionary. Skinner's major work *The Foundations of Modern Political Thought* (1978) reconstructed the main political arguments of the later sixteenth century so as to show how certain foundational ideas for modern political thought came to be defined and articulated at that time. Pocock was perhaps responsible for the most dramatic breakthrough. He was able to show in works such as *The Machiavellian Moment* that the way most historians had understood the political and social thought of the seventeenth and eighteenth centuries was profoundly anachronistic. Authors such as G. H. Sabine or Isaac Kramnick argued that this period was marked by the gradual appearance of modern political ideologies such as liberalism, which were associated with social groups such as the bourgeoisie (hence Kramnick's emphasis in his works on 'bourgeois radicalism'). Pocock argued convincingly that the arguments and ideas that later historians had understood as liberal or proto-liberal were actually employing a different vocabulary, that of 'republicanism' or 'civic humanism', which had quite different concerns and was reactive and backward-looking rather than optimistic and future oriented. Historians had literally not understood what people from those periods were talking about.[11]

From our position today, we can now see that the innovations of Skinner, Dunn and Pocock have had a permanent effect, which is now spreading outside the original area of the history of political thought. The strongly **teleological** approach of earlier works has largely gone, as has the sub-Marxist emphasis upon economic and social structure as a determinant of belief. The contextualist methodology set out in Skinner's articles is the most influential by far among current practitioners. One consequence is an interest in a much wider range of sources, including works once dismissed as 'minor' or 'secondary'. These are now seen as more useful because of their very typicality and lack of originality. There is an effort to recover and understand forms of argument and thought that have previously been ignored or not recognized. One major change that can be traced back to the work of the 'Cambridge School' is a greater awareness of the importance of religious ideas and assumptions for the intellectual history of most of the historic past. The idea of a steady movement to secularization since the seventeenth century is now widely rejected. There is now a sensitivity to the risk of reading secular ways of thinking backwards into the past or of giving sceptical ideas greater prominence than is actually justified. Ideas and systems of belief outside the narrowly political are also attracting attention with study of such topics as nineteenth-century ideas about poverty and charity. The intellectual history of the early modern period now sees more attention being paid to belief systems such as magic, hermeticism, millenarianism and prophecy. One result of this has been to derail much of the older account of the rise of science. Historians are now much more aware of the connection and overlap between science and magic. Isaac Newton, for example, is now seen more as he was, interested in alchemy and hermeticism as well as mechanics, rather than as the modern scientist of traditional historiography.

The 'new intellectual history' is in some ways more difficult to practise, not least because it requires much more reading! However, it is more productive as far as historians are concerned. One of its results is to rule out certain ways of reading historical texts and the ideas expressed in them as being useful *for historians*. It is perfectly reasonable for political philosophers to read Locke from the perspective of twentieth-century analytical philosophy. Historians, however, are interested in discovering what he was trying to say in the seventeenth century, how he was understood by his contemporaries, and where his ideas and arguments came from. The are also interested in tracing how later generations understood his arguments and how these readings differed from the ones he was actually making at the time he wrote his works. It is much easier to do these things following the kind of methodology described earlier.

▶ Critics and sceptics

Of course, all of this has its critics among both historians and philosophers. Revealingly, it is the latter who are more discomfited. As Skinner himself remarks, the criticisms come from all points of the intellectual compass. Fortunately, his main methodological works and a representative sample of his critics have been assembled in one book, *Meaning and Context: Quentin Skinner and his Critics* (1988), edited by James Tully. One critic, Kenneth Minogue, argues that his approach is too historically minded and theoretical, and trivializes the study of ideas. Another, Joseph Femia, argues that he is not historicist enough from a Gramscian perspective.[12] The criticisms reveal indirectly the nature of the argument they attack. It is essentially the application of empirical historical reasoning to the slippery topic of history of ideas. Many historians have made this point. In doing so they tend to downplay the significance of the methodological writings of Skinner, Pocock and Dunn. David Wooton remarks:

> The last two decades, it is generally agreed, have seen major changes in the study of the history of political thought, and there has been much talk of a 'revolution' inaugurated by Quentin Skinner's 1969 essay 'Meaning and Understanding in the History of Ideas'. In large part, however, these changes are the result of lengthy evolution, rather than the heroic deeds of a vanguard partly guided by correct theory. They represent merely the application of the methods and values of professional history to the history of ideas.[13]

Sir Geoffrey Elton, in the course of his blast against the postmodernists, said:

> Skinner has told us repeatedly that if we want to know what Machiavelli or Hobbes meant – what they were trying to say – we have to gain as perfect a grasp as possible of their own language and the setting – historical, ideological, possibly economic and biological, and certainly political – within which they worked. Because they were thinking from within their own world, we have to follow them into that world. But this is surely just the general recipe for coming to grips with the past, and when Skinner put his doctrines to work, especially in his *Foundations of Modern Political Thought* (1978), he seemed to me to produce excellent and pellucid examples of what ever since the work of John Neville Figgis in the 1890s has been the best procedure for historians of political thought, and by implication of such other forms of intellectual history as that of literature and science.[14]

Obviously this is true up to a point. The work of Figgis, mentioned by Elton, does indeed show many of the methodological features championed by Skinner, particularly his *Divine Right of Kings* (1896). However, the argument that what Dunn, Pocock and Skinner advocated was what historians had been doing anyway is to miss the point. This was what they had been doing in other areas, but not so much in the area of history of ideas. Here the influence of other disciplines, particularly philosophy and literary criticism, was so great that a formal statement of a methodological programme was probably necessary to bring about a widespread change in practice.

▶ Other types of intellectual history

Outside the English-speaking world there have been other developments with a more ambiguous relationship to empirical methods. German historiography has its own tradition of intellectual history, with prominent figures such as Herbert Grundman (1902–1970). More recent years have seen the approach usually known as *Begriffsgeschichte*, which is associated with Reinhard Kosseleck. This is the historical study of complex concepts, such as 'God', which combine or involve many other ideas and act as categories that organize thought. In some ways this is an inversion of Lovejoy's notion of the unit idea. Koselleck's own work has concentrated on an area of continuing interest to German and French intellectual historians, the Enlightenment of the eighteenth century and its effects and origins.[15]

Cultural history of the type pioneered by Burckhardt continued steadily throughout the twentieth century, including such famous works as *The Waning of the Middle Ages* (1919) and *Dutch Civilisation in the Seventeenth Century* (1938) by Johan Huizinga (1872–1945). The most important kind of cultural history for intellectual history has been the *Histoire de mentalités*, effectively created by French historians as a distinctive type of historiography. The 'founding father' was Lucien Fèbvre (1878–1956), one of the founders (with Marc Bloch) of the journal *Annales*. *Histoire de mentalités* is concerned to recover the attitudes, outlooks, beliefs and habits of thought of the population at large as well as of individuals. It is concerned with the mental furniture (mental apparatus or *outillage mental* in Fèbvre's phrase) of people in the past rather than elaborately articulated arguments. Historians in this area are interested in such things as the conceptions of time or death and other kinds of human experience held by people in the past. Fèbvre himself explored the mental world of the French writer Rabelais, concluding that it was not possible to be an atheist in sixteenth-century France because the mental tools needed to formulate such a position did not exist.[16]

The history of *mentalités* is sometimes seen as an alternative to empirical history. Sometimes it can be, as when theoretical constructs such as ideal types are made to drive the analysis or when the research is structured by a concern other than that of exploring the past. However, in this as in other areas, it is not the subject matter but the method of investigation that makes the historiography empirical or non-empirical. Fèbvre's work on Rabelais was strictly empirical in its method and the same is true of other work of this kind. There can be an empirical history of *mentalités* just as there can be an empirical history of ideas in general.

History of ideas is undoubtedly the area where empirical research faces its greatest challenge. It is also the topic where historians share much subject matter with other disciplines, such as literary studies. The evidence so far suggests that empirical methods are now the predominant pattern for investigation in this as in other areas, and that fears of infection from the methodologies of other disciplines can be discounted.

Conclusion

Empirical history is a way of thinking, studying and writing about the human past. It came into being in the early modern period, became established and institutionalized during the nineteenth century, and went on to become a veritable academic industry during the twentieth century. This way of thinking about the past is a prominent feature of the modern world. The empirical approach to the past is one of the central elements of the *mentalité* of the modern man or woman, distinguishing them from many of their predecessors. In the past other ways of thinking about and understanding the past were predominant, such as **myth**, tradition and epic. These might then be explored using reasoned argument but the 'authority' remained the ultimate source of knowledge, however it was extended using exegesis and **hermeneutics**. As with other areas of human thought, the last 400 years have seen a move away from answering questions about the world and our place in it by reference to revealed religion, authoritative texts or religious and other kinds of tradition. Instead, the stress is on investigation employing both reasoned argument and investigation of the physical world using the human senses. Today, in what some would have us believe is the 'late modern' or even **'postmodern'** era, this way of gaining understanding of the world is under attack, in history as elsewhere.

The appearance and elaboration of empirical history has had important effects. It has changed the way people think about the past and their response to statements made about it. We can now ask about any statement made concerning the past: 'Is it true?' It has led to much greater knowledge of the past. A contemporary historian of the ancient world will know more about the Roman Empire than Gibbon did. This is often doubted but the examples given earlier confirm this. We now know much more about, for example, how households were organized in early modern Europe or the living standards and incomes of nineteenth-century workers than we did even 50 years ago. Part of this growth of knowledge is 'negative' rather than 'positive'. Rather than learning things that we did not know before, we have discovered that things we thought we knew are not so certain. An important aspect of this is the way empirical investigation of the past has undermined many received myths. Many national myths, such as the idea of the Anglo-Saxon roots of English liberty, have been swept away. Empirical research has also dissolved other 'replacement myths' such as the idea of 'revolutionary England' or the **narrative** of 'progress'. Narrative is a central part of empirical history, but it has proved impossible to sustain any kind of 'grand narrative' of history (national or otherwise) in the face of the complexity and detail produced by empirical research.

However, this way of studying the past has been under attack from the moment it was defined. The idea of the search for truth as the historian's goal has been attacked by those making the case for history as **advocacy**, from the nineteenth-century 'Prussian School' to contemporary figures such as Beverley Southgate.[1] Others have argued for the historian as a creator rather than discoverer, an author/creator instead of a researcher. The case for historical **relativism** and radical **scepticism** about ever truly knowing anything significant has been put by a series of authors, from Renaissance **Pyrrhonists** to contemporary postmodernists. Others have argued for the vital role of explicit **theory** in history, with theories shaping and directing the investigation rather than being mere **heuristic** devices.

Despite this, the most dramatic feature of empirical history is its persistence. As the examples given earlier in the book show, the empirical approach has remained the dominant one over a wide range of topics and has beaten off strong challenges in several areas. Even avowed critics of empirical history often turn out in their own work to be as empirical as the next historian in their actual methods. One possible explanation is institutional inertia. The establishment of history as a profession based in the modern university, with the apparatus of reviews, **learned journals** and conferences, has perhaps created a powerful set of incentives to study and write in a certain way in order to gain career success. However, this seems an inadequate explanation, given the success by these criteria of people who have denied any support for traditional methods, and the predilection of the modern world for novelty.

There are several other explanations both for the persistence of empiricism and the recurring attacks on it. One is mutual incomprehension between different disciplines as to what it is they are actually doing or trying to do in their professional capacity. A problem in Anglophone countries is the distinctive English understanding of the word '**science**'. The equivalent term in most languages (*Wissenschaft* in German for example) has the same meaning as the original word '*scientia*', that is, any kind of systematic or structured knowledge that is gained by organized, systematic study. 'Science' in this sense is contrasted to 'art' or 'literature' and includes disciplines such as history. In the Anglophone world, however, 'science' means a particular kind of systematic study, specifically one that is based upon repeatable controlled experiments and generates general laws. This effectively limits the term to a few subjects such as physics. Claims that empirical history is scientific are ridiculed (correctly) when the term is understood in its narrow, English sense. It makes perfect sense when used in its wider meaning. In general, philosophers and literary scholars have had a hard time understanding what it is that historians actually do, or try to do. For their part, historians often show a wilful obtuseness about philosophical arguments. There are good reasons for academic specialization.

One repeated misunderstanding in criticisms of the dominant historical method is a failure to grasp the difference between aims and intentions and what is actually achieved. Because empirical historians produce work that is clearly influenced by their own historical location, it does not follow that they should not *try* to be disinterested and detached, nor that the impossibility of achieving 100 per cent detachment means the only alternative is zero per cent. Historians who try to be disinterested are likely to be closer to that goal than those who do not. Of course, there is the view that this attempt is not only doomed to fail but morally reprehensible. People who take this position ultimately deny that truth, however approximate and imperfect, is the goal of the historian – or any other researcher.

Perhaps the most common cause of misunderstanding, among historians themselves, is the failure to distinguish between subject matter and method. There is a persistent tendency to identify empiricism (a method) with a specific kind of subject matter, or a certain style of writing and rhetoric. When a new subject matter or analytical technique is introduced, this is then seen or presented as a movement away from empiricism. So, for example, the development of cultural history in the later nineteenth century and the introduction of macroeconomic analysis and statistics (**cliometrics**) into economic history in the 1960s were both presented as assaults on naïve empiricism. In reality, phenomena like these simply show the application of empirical research to new areas of the human past or the refining and improving of empirical method. The individual historians who introduce the method usually turn out to be traditional in most of their actual methods and assumptions. The new subject area is typically launched with claims that it will transform the whole discipline of history (this claim has been made for cliometrics, women's history and social history, among others), but after a few years settles down as an established sub-discipline, with its own apparatus of journals and conferences. It is still connected to the other parts of the discipline – by shared methodological assumptions that turn out to be broadly empirical.

The persistence and resilience of empirical methods can be seen in several of the examples looked at earlier, particularly political and economic history. History of ideas shows how this way of studying the past continues to spread, to topics that might seem unsuitable. The final reason for this perhaps is that other approaches to history are ultimately disappointing in their results, given the dominant idea of the purpose of intellectual endeavour. There are other ways of studying and understanding the past than empirical history. One can set out to create myth or an inspiring story or something passionate or beautiful. In other words, one can follow a literary or mythical approach. In many ways this is reasonable and helpful. It is not true that good history must be uninteresting, badly written or uninspiring. Literary and rhetorical skills are important parts of what makes a good historian. However, these are subordinate to the primary aim of discovering the truth. A historian may aim to write a work that is moving and has an effect in the historian's own world and time, but this must never be at the expense of truth and cannot involve invention or speculation. So, these cannot be the primary purpose of the exercise. Since at least the seventeenth century the principal aim for most academic endeavours has been to make statements about the world that can withstand the question: 'But is it true?' The answer to that question for the historian should be 'yes' or (more often), 'yes, as far as we know, and here is why'. This process of question and answer is much easier when the agreed method of settling questions of truth and explanation is by appeal to physical evidence, that is, by empirical methods. The problem with alternatives such as Collingwood's re-enactment is their subjective quality, which makes it very difficult to establish which of several competing truth-claims has a better basis. Of course, one can take the postmodernist or Pyrrhonist path of abandoning the idea of truth but most historians, for very good reasons, are not prepared to do this. Consequently, they are driven back to empirical methods. This will be true so long as history is defined, in however qualified a way, as being about knowledge.[2]

History develops in part from the crisis of Renaissance **scepticism** and the breakdown of religious authority in the Reformation. It is one part of the wider movement towards an investigative, critical approach to understanding the world. The overwhelming majority of historians remain committed to this in various ways.[3] That is why they also remain broadly empiricist.

Glossary

Advocacy Applied to history, the belief that the purpose of history as an activity is the study of the past in order to make an argument or case for something regarded as good in the historian's own time, for example the 'Prussian School' of German historians saw the point of their endeavours to be the creation of support for a united Germany and the policy and institutions of the Prussian state.

Anachronism Literally 'misplaced in time'. The faulty ascription of qualities, knowledge, behaviour that are appropriate and correct for one period of time to another where they are not. Having John Locke think like a nineteenth-century liberal is an example. Most anachronism comes from reading the present or more recent past backwards into the more distant past.

Antiquarianism The study of the past as an exercise in accumulating a body of facts about an aspect of it. Unlike history it does not involve the attempt to *explain* the past. Appears as an activity in the sixteenth century.

A posteriori A form of reasoning that starts after experience has led to knowledge. Associated with **inductive reasoning**.

A priori A form of reasoning that starts with knowledge or assumes it before physical experience. Associated with **deductive reasoning**.

Argument from authority An argument in the form 'X is true because Y says so' where Y is a person or text that is held to be authoritative. Opposed to the argument from evidence or experience where a statement is held to be true because it corresponds to experience or evidence of some kind.

Auteur French term meaning 'author/artist'. In **historiography** historians are seen as '*auteurs*' by thinkers such as Collingwood and Croce, who see the historian as *creating* meaning through the forming of a **narrative**, rather than as *discovering* it by a process of empirical investigation.

Belles lettres Non-fiction writing of a literary kind. Used particularly of essays and literary criticism.

Chorography A type of **antiquarianism** that seeks to uncover all of the information about a particular location/place.

Chronology The study of the relation of different events to each other in time so that they can be put into a sequence with respect to a particular event taken as a starting point (such as the birth of Jesus, the flight of Muhammad to Medina or the foundation of Rome). Something we take for granted that is actually very difficult and absolutely essential for the practice of history.

Citation The practice of telling the reader of a work of history where the evidence for an assertion or argument could be found. This told the reader, among other things, if a statement was derived from a primary or secondary source and whether a quote or paraphrase from another text was accurate.

Cliometrics Quantitative economic history. More generally, the application of economic models to the study of the past and the use of analytical categories such as 'national income' derived from macroeconomics.

Coherence theory of truth Holds that statements are true if they are internally coherent or command general assent from similar observers (sometimes called consensus theory of truth). Contrasted with the correspondence theory of truth.

Conflict/consensus theories of politics The two predominant theories of the nature of politics in modern political science. They differ over what the normal (or in computing terminology 'default') condition of politics is and hence the nature of politics. In conflict theory, conflict and disagreement is the norm and politics is the activity of managing or resolving that conflict. For consensus theory, co-operation is the norm and politics is the process of co-operation. They are important for historians because they lead to different conclusions about what kind of events are unusual and require explanation.

Correspondence theory of truth Holds that statements are true either by virtue of the definitions of the words used in them (for example, an odd number is not even) or because it corresponds to a physical feature of the world that we know via perception.

Counterfactual An argument of the form: 'If event X had not happened or had taken a different form, then the actual known course of events Y would have been significantly different.' For example, 'If the Spanish Armada had landed, it would have succeeded and England would have become a part of the Spanish Empire.' In science fiction the basis of the popular 'alternative history' sub-genre as practised by authors such as Harry Turtledove. In history, all judgements as to the relative importance or unimportance of individuals or events rest upon an implicit counter-factual. The difficulty is that it is theoretically impossible to establish the truth or falsity of a counterfactual **hypothesis**.

Deduction   The opposite of **induction**. Reasoning from a premiss known or assumed to be true to a specific conclusion.

Dialectic   A form of argument, also a type of process of change, in which a thesis is opposed to its contradictory antithesis. The two are then reconciled with each other in the 'higher' synthesis. Associated in particular with the philosophy of Hegel and with Marxism, via the concept of **dialectical materialism**.

Dialectical materialism   The name given to the historical analysis of Marx, which combined a materialist form of analysis with the dialectical understanding of the process of change. The critical difference from the Hegelian model was that the elements (thesis, antithesis, synthesis) were seen not as Ideas but as material forces, specifically the organization of the productive process.

Diplomatics   The study of documents, looking at the regular features of content, structure, language and internal organization of texts produced by an institution or even (sometimes) an individual.

Empiricism   A doctrine of **epistemology** which holds that sense experience is the source of knowledge. Associated with **induction** and the **correspondence theory of truth**.

Enlightenment   An intellectual movement found throughout Europe in the later eighteenth century but particularly in Scotland, France, and Germany. Associated with scepticism about religious belief, confidence in the power of reason, a belief in progress and in the idea of a universal human nature.

Epigraphy   The study of inscriptions on stone or some other hard medium. A vital source for ancient history.

Epiphenomenon   Literally 'surface phenomenon'. An entity or phenomenon that exists only as a consequence or secondary feature of another 'deeper' phenomenon. In **historiography** it is often argued or assumed that phenomena such as culture or politics are epiphenomena of something else, usually economic relations and organization.

Epistemology The branch of philosophy that deals with questions of knowledge, what we can know and how we know it.

Erudits 'The learned ones'. A mocking term invented in the eighteenth century to describe antiquarian scholars. Now used as a neutral term for such people.

Etymology The study of the origins and history of words and their meaning.

Fact A **truth statement** that has had its truth confirmed to some degree.

Fallibilism A form of moderate scepticism which holds that we should always hold truth statements to be true in a tentative sense, that is, as being capable of being disproved, but also that the degree of tentativeness can vary and we can by investigation move statements from the less certain to more certain category.

Hagiography Strictly speaking, the lives of saints. More loosely, any kind of biography that is uncritical and presents its subject in constantly glowing colours.

Hermeneutics The study of texts so as to uncover new or concealed meanings within the text or to reconcile apparent contradictions within the same text or between texts written by the same author. Originally developed for the study of scripture or legal documents, but now applied more widely by literary scholars and philosophers. Often confused with the search for **'unwitting testimony'** by historians, but in fact an ahistorical method.

Heuristic A proposition or **hypothesis** that generates a programme of research or investigation by suggesting what might be best to look for, but does not predict exactly what will be found or what conclusions will be arrived at.

Historicism A set of ideas about the past and its study that was formulated in nineteenth-century Germany. The central idea is that the past must be understood in its own terms and that no part of the past has a particularly privileged or significant position. In its extreme form this can lead to **relativism**.

Historiography: What historians have written about the past. The systematic study of those writings.

History The systematic, evidence-based study of the human past. *Not* the past itself.

Hypothesis A statement about the world that is put forward as a tentative suggestion rather than as a definite **truth statement**. It can then become the starting point for investigation which may, by **induction**, confirm, disprove or amend it.

Humanism An intellectual movement of the Renaissance, devoted to the rediscovery of classical ideas and learning and especially the humane studies (as opposed to theology).

Idealism The doctrine that knowledge comes not only from sensory experience, but also from the structure of the human mind so that some things can be known without experience or before it.

Ideal type A methodological device in sociology, devised by the German sociologist Max Weber. It is a composite combining the features found in most specific instance of a phenomenon (such as a city), but does not exactly correspond to any particular real case.

Illocutionary meaning The meaning given to a **speech act** by such factors as its location, time and context.

Incommensurable Applied to two or more entities when there is no other neutral or universal standard by which they can be compared or assessed. For followers of the extreme **historicism** of Dilthey, different historical epochs and cultures are incommensurable.

Induction A process of reasoning from specific cases to general conclusions or **hypotheses**.

Intuition The phenomenon of the (alleged) immediate gaining of knowledge or understanding by the mind, without resort to either reason or experience.

Jurisprudence The study of the theory and philosophy of law, both as abstract idea and as embodied in historic legal institutions and practices.

Knowledge The body of **truth statements** that can be made about the world or some aspect of it.

Learned journal A regular publication, devoted to a particular academic dis-cipline or (more frequently) a part or aspect of that discipline, which publishes pieces based upon original research and reviewed for publication by other scholars, as well as reviewing and assessing books and other publications. An essential institution of the modern academy, invented in nineteenth-century Germany.

Locutionary meaning The meaning of a **speech act** that comes from the established meaning of the words (or gestures, symbols, etc.) employed in it.

Maurists The Congregation of Saint Maur, a monastic establishment in France that played a major part in the growth of **diplomatics** and the systematic study of records.

Myth For historians an account of the past that has an element of truth, or makes use of facts but is largely untrue, or employs the true elements in a narrative the point of which is false. One of the effects of history is to reveal which accounts of the past are mythical. Thus, the idea of an 'ancient constitution' was shown to be a myth by nineteenth-century historians of Britain.

Narrative An account of past events, often, but not always in chronological order, that seeks to explain how and why things happened in the way that they did. In other words, a way of studying historical causation. *Not* a story in the literary sense, despite what some may say.

Nominalism The doctrine that universals (words or concepts that refer to classes or categories such as 'cat') have no real existence, they do not refer to anything concrete. Instead, they are labels of convenience used to make reasoning easier. In history this would mean that concepts such as 'class' or 'feudalism' do not exist as such: it is the particular things they refer to that exist.

Numismatics The scientific study of coins. Important for ancient historians for whom coins are a very important primary source.

Ontology The branch of philosophy that deals with questions of existence.

Palaeography The systematic study of documents, looking at such features as the nature and date of the material, the nature of the handwriting and so on.

Past The totality of those things that we perceive as having already been.

Philology The study of words, their meanings, origins, how they get their meanings and how these change over time.

Positivism Correctly, means the idea that there can be a science of human society with the same qualities as the natural sciences, particularly the discovery of universal laws which, as well as explaining the past and present, will predict the future. Misused by some authors to mean strict **empiricism** as opposed to a more theoretical approach. What they are actually talking about is **induction**.

Postmodernism   A body of ideas derived from literary studies and philosophy of language that denies the possibility of true knowledge or (in the more extreme versions) of a reality independent of language.

Premiss   A factual statement of some kind which is assumed to be true and then made the starting point for an argument using one of the forms of logic.

Presentism   The idea that history is or should be shaped by the concerns and interests of the historian's own time. Also used to describe historiography where this is clearly the case, even when the historian in question does not intend this.

Primary sources   Evidence for events or people (such as documents, coins, inscriptions) that are produced directly by the event or person, or very closely in space and time. Contrasted to **secondary sources**.

Prosopography   The practice of compiling a collective biography of a group of people who share some important feature (such as legislators) by establishing a range of facts about each individual life and then seeing if patterns can be discerned. Associated with the English historian Sir Lewis Namier.

Providence   The idea that everything that happens in the world is doing so according to a divine purpose and conforms to a pattern reflecting that purpose, even if we cannot fully discern it.

Psychoanalysis   The theories about human psychology and motivation put forward by Freud. Also the therapeutic practice based on those ideas.

Pyrrhonism   An extreme form of scepticism first formulated by the Greek philosopher Pyrrho, but known mainly through the later writer Sextus Empiricus. Holds that we cannot truly know anything about the world because of the unreliability of both senses and reason.

Rationalism   Generally speaking, the belief that reason is a reliable means for establishing the truth. Historically, the belief, found widely during the **Enlightenment**, that reason was to be preferred to revealed religion, tradition or authority as a source of knowledge and guidance on how to live.

Referent   In **philology** the object or idea to which a word refers.

Regius An adjective applied to certain academic posts in Britain, meaning that the appointment is in the gift of the Crown (actually the Prime Minister).

Relativism A word with many meanings. In general, the doctrine that such things as knowledge, truth, beauty, and so on are not absolute but relative, that is, there is no universal or objective standard in such matters by which we may judge particular cases. In **historiography**, the idea that there are no universal principles such as a human nature which are applicable to all times and places.

Romanticism A cultural and intellectual movement of nineteenth-century Europe that was a reaction to the ideas of the **Enlightenment**. It emphasised emotion rather than reason and communities of sentiment such as nations. In **historiography** associated with the idea of history as a kind of art or advocacy, the aim of which was to evoke feelings in the reader. Michelet is perhaps the quintessential Romantic historian.

Scepticism A philosophical position about the possibility of knowledge. In its moderate form that we can know things only in a tentative way or under strict conditions. In its extreme form the argument that nothing is knowable (see **Pyrrhonism**). As a method of investigation of the world, the principle that we should take nothing for granted or as true on **authority** but should subject all statements to scrutiny.

Science In most languages any systematic, structured body of knowledge and the discipline that leads to the discovery and acquiring of that knowledge. History is a science of this sort. In English a way of acquiring knowledge with very specific qualities, such as the use of controlled, repeatable experiments. History is not a science in this sense.

Secondary sources Things that give information about a historical person or event that are produced after the event or by a person at some remove either spatially or chronologically. The writings of historians are typically secondary sources but can be **primary sources** for the time when they were produced and may become primary sources if all of the original evidence is lost, as is the case with many ancient writers.

Sources The raw material of history. Specifically, the physical remains of the past, such as records, coins, inscriptions and artefacts from which we gain our knowledge of it. Divided into **primary** and **secondary**.

Speech act A concept taken from the philosophy of A. L. Austin and used by Quentin Skinner. Any act (such as speech, acting, publication, broadcasting) that conveys meaning and information from the person who performs the act to others (the audience). See **locutionary** and **illocutionary meaning**.

Stadial 'In stages'. In historiography the idea that human history consists of a series of sequential stages of development, each in some sense 'higher' or more 'developed' than its predecessor. A very common idea, found for example in both Adam Smith and Karl Marx.

Structuralist In historiography, the belief that the outcome of historical processes is largely determined or shaped by social and economic structures, that is, patterns of organization and behaviour, rather than by either contingent chance or human choice. Associated particularly with the *Annales* school of French historians but common elsewhere.

Teleology The idea that history is a movement towards an end state or goal (in Greek *telos*). It was in this sense that Fukuyama spoke of the 'end' of history. Marxism is a teleological model of history.

Theory Used in history in two slightly different ways. First, it means a **hypothesis** or tentative explanation, put forward on the basis of what is known so far, that helps the historian to organize or make sense of their findings and suggests a pattern of further research. Theories of this sort are subject to revision or discarding if the research produces information that does not fit. Second, to mean a systematic, structured argument about the nature of humans, society or some aspect of history, which has a predictive quality and is known to be true before further research. Here the aim of research is not to test the theory but to confirm it, as the theory tells the researcher what to look for, what she will find and how to understand it.

Truth statement A statement about the world, that can be shown to be true or false. Some are capable of being true *a priori* (before investigation) by virtue of the definition of the terms they use. Others can be shown to be true *a posteriori* (after investigation). The issue dividing philosophers is that of how one determines if a statement is indeed true.

Universalism A feature of **Enlightenment** thought. The belief that ultimately all human beings shared a common nature and that therefore all human societies past and present could be understood in the same way, using the same analytical concepts. In history leads to an emphasis on studying mankind in general rather than particular places.

Unwitting testimony A term formulated by Arthur Marwick. It means the information that a historian can get from a historical record that the original author did not *intend* to put into it. Most of the information that historians get from records is of this type.

Verstehen Broadly means 'empathy'. In the thought of Dilthey and Max Weber the idea that in the study of human beings the investigator (historian or sociologist) can and should seek to identify emotionally and mentally with the object of their study. Only then will they be able to see the world as the object does and so truly understand them. This means rejection of the idea of detachment. In history leads to the influential theory of Collingwood, which sees historians as engaged in re-enacting the past events they are studying.

Whig history In the narrow sense a way of looking at the history of the British constitution that saw it as a process leading up to the modern British state, so that the earlier forms of the institutions were seen only as forerunners of the later ones and not in their own terms, as they were understood at the time. In general, any approach to history that sees the past mainly in terms of the way it became the present.

Zeitgeist The 'spirit of the age'. The common ideas, beliefs and ways of thinking of a particular historical period.

Notes

▶ Introduction

1   John Tosh, *The Pursuit of History*, 2nd edn (London: Longmans, 1991), pp. 130–51, 236.

2   Sir Geoffrey Elton, *Return to Essentials: Some Reflections on the Present State of Historical Study* (Cambridge: Cambridge University Press, 1991), p. 41.

3   Richard Evans, *In Defence of History* (London: Granta, 1997). Keith Windschuttle, *The Killing of History: How Literary Critics and Social Theorists are Murdering Our Past* (New York: Free Press, 1996). Arthur Marwick, *The New Nature of History: Knowledge, Evidence, Language* (Basingstoke: Palgrave – now Palgrave Macmillan, 2001). For the postmodernists side of the argument, see Keith Jenkins (ed.), *The Postmodern History Reader* (London: Routledge, 1997), and *Re-Thinking History* (London: Routledge, 1991). Alan Munslow, *The Routledge Companion to Historical Studies* (London: Routledge, 1991), and *Deconstructing History* (London: Routledge, 1997).

4   Technically this is an argument of the form 'All As are B. C is an A. Therefore C is B', a syllogism of mood Barbara.

5   The 'fallibilistic' approach to knowledge statements and the idea of a movement from lesser to greater certainty without ever arriving at total certainty are associated with the American philosopher Charles Sanders Pierce (1839–1914). See Richard H. Popkin (ed.), *The Pimlico History of Western Philosophy* (London: Pimlico, 1999), pp. 592–9.

6   For a defence of induction with specific reference to history, see Windschuttle, *Killing of History*, pp. 211–15.

7   Ludmilla Jordanova, *History in Practice* (London: Arnold, 2000) pp. 91–113 and especially pp. 111–12.

8   Hayden White, *Metahistory: The Historical Imagination in Nineteenth Century Europe* (Baltimore: Johns Hopkins University Press, 1973), and *The Content of the Form* (Baltimore: Johns Hopkins University Press, 1987).

9   R. G. Collingwood, *The Idea of History*, ed. J. Van der Dussen (Oxford: Oxford University Press, 1994) 1st edn 1946. Michael Oakeshott, *On History and Other Essays* (Indianapolis: Liberty Fund, 2000) 1st edn 1983. Benedetto Croce, *History as the Story of Liberty* (Indianapolis: Liberty Fund, 2001) 1st edn 1941.

John Lukács, *Historical Consciousness: The Remembered Past* (Englewood Cliffs, NJ: Transaction Publishers, 1994).

10   Quoted in J. P. Kenyon, *The History Men* 2nd edn (London: Weidenfield & Nicolson, 1993), p. 124.

11   See, for example, Jean E. Howard, 'Towards a postmodern historical practice', in Francis Barker, Peter Hulme and Margaret Iverson (eds), *Uses of History: Marxism, Postmodernism and the Renaissance* (Manchester: Manchester University Press, 1991), pp. 101–22 'Such writing, of course, will not yield us the truth of the past or present, but it might yield a knowledge adequate to the political needs of present struggles' (p. 121).

▶ 1   The Creation of Empirical History

1   A good discussion of this can be found in Joseph M. Levine, *Humanism and History: Origins of Modern English Historiography* (Ithaca, NY: Cornell University Press, 1987). See especially the first chapter 'Caxton's histories: Fact and fiction at the close of the Middle Ages', pp. 19–53.

2   F. S. Fussner, *The Historical Revolution: English Historical Writing and Thought 1580–1640* (London: Routledge & Kegan Paul, 1962). See also Joseph H. Preston, 'Was there an historical revolution?', *Journal of the History of Ideas*, XXXVIII (1977), 353–64.

3   Donald R. Kelley, *Foundations of Modern Historical Scholarship: Language, Law and History in the French Renaissance* (New York: Columbia University Press, 1970), pp. 19–52 looks at Valla and his work. For a different perspective, see Linda G. Janik, 'Lorenzo Valla: The primacy of rhetoric and the demoralization of history', *History and Theory*, XII (1973), 389–404.

4   For a succinct account of Renaissance Pyrrhonism, see Popkin, *Pimlico History of Western Philosophy*, pp. 329–36.

5   For a discussion of Bacon's theories as applied to history, see A. Guibbory 'Francis Bacon's view of history: The cycles of error and the progress of truth' *Journal of English and Germanic Philology*, LXXIV (1975), 336–50.

6   'Francogallia' was one of many works of this kind published during the sixteenth-century wars of religion in France. The use of history in these 'monarchomach' tracts, produced by both Catholic and Protestant authors, is discussed in Quentin Skinner, *The Foundations of Modern Political Thought*, 2 vols (Cambridge: Cambridge University Press, 1978).

7   Donald R. Kelley, 'The rise of legal history in the Renaissance', *History and Theory*, IX (1970), 174–94, and also 'Legal humanism and the sense of history', *Studies in the Renaissance*, XIII (1966), 184–99.

8   Kelley, *Foundations of Modern Historical Scholarship*, is the major work in this area. See particularly Part 2 of the work, pp. 53–150.

9 Ibid., pp. 116–50. See also Denys Hay, *Annalists and Historians: Western Historiography From the Eighth to the Eighteenth Centuries* (London: Methuen, 1977), pp. 127–32 (the relevant passage from Sidney is quoted on p. 128).

10 For Bodin's work, see Julian H. Franklin, *Jean Bodin and the Sixteenth-Century Revolution in the Methodology of Law and History* (New York: Columbia University Press, 1961). See also John H. Arnold, *History: A Very Short Introduction* (Oxford: Oxford University Press, 2000), pp. 29–31.

11 Fussner, *The Historical Revolution*, gives a detailed account of English antiquarianism in this period. See also Levine, *Humanism and History*, ch. 3 'The antiquarian enterprise, 1500–1800', pp. 73–106. The classic account of historical thought at this time is J. G. A. Pocock, *The Ancient Constitution and the Feudal Law: A Study of English Historical thought in the Seventeenth Century* 2nd edn (Cambridge: Cambridge University Press, 1987).

12 See Hay, *Annalists and Historians*, pp. 132–85.

13 For Clarendon and Burnet, see Kenyon, *The History Men*, pp. 31–40.

14 For an interesting and stimulating study of this kind of historiography, see Mark Salber Phillips, *Society and Sentiment: Genres of Historical Writing in Britain, 1740–1820* (Princeton, NJ: Princeton University Press, 2000). See also Arnold, *History*, pp. 46–52.

15 Hume's work is now readily available in an inexpensive edition and repays reading as an example of style (the term urbane could have been invented for him). See David Hume, *The History of England from the Invasion of Julius Caesar to the Revolution in 1688*, 6 vols (Indianapolis: Liberty Fund, 1983) reprint of 1778 edition.

16 Ferguson has benefited from his status as a founding father of sociology by having his work made available in modern editions. See Adam Ferguson, *An Essay on the History of Civil Society* (New Brunswick, NJ: Transaction 1990). By contrast, Kames, despite his importance for cultural history, has received much less attention. See Phillips, *Society and Sentiment*, pp. 108–10, 173–9.

17 For what is still the best account of Millar, see W. C. Lehman, *John Millar of Glasgow* (Cambridge: Cambridge University Press, 1960).

18 John Warren, *The Past and its Presenters: An Introduction to Issues in Historiography* (London: Hodder & Stoughton, 1998), pp. 92–104.

19 For Gibbon's position as an historian, see Arnaldo Momigliano, 'Gibbon's contribution to historical method', in *Studies in Historiography* (London: Weidenfield & Nicolson, 1966); and Roy Porter, *Edward Gibbon: Making History* (London: 1988). Gibbon's location in the intellectual world of his time and his use of the ideas and concepts developed by others is explored in J. G. A. Pocock, *Barbarism and Religion: Vol. I The Enlightenments of Edward Gibbon; Vol. II Narratives of Civil Government* (Cambridge: Cambridge University Press, 2001).

▶ 2 The Perfection of Empirical History

1 George Peabody Gooch, *History and Historians in the Nineteenth Century* (London: Longmans, Green & Co., 1913), pp. 10–13.

2 The literature on Ranke is immense. The following are a starting point. Gooch, *History and Historians*, pp. 76–129. Peter Gay, *Style in History* (London: Johathan Cape, 1975), pp. 59–94. G. G. Iggers and J. M. Powell (eds), *Leopold Von Ranke and the Shaping of the Historical Discipline* (Syracuse, NY: Syracuse University Press, 1990). G. G. Iggers and K. Von Moltke (eds), *The Theory and Practice of History* (Indianapolis: Bobbs-Merrill, 1973). In addition to the last work it is still worth looking at some of the great man's works themselves. See, for example, Leopold Von Ranke, *The Ottoman and Spanish Monarchies in the Sixteenth and Seventeenth Centuries*, trans. W. K. Kelly (London: Whittaker, 1843), and *History of the Popes, Their Church and State*, trans. E. Foster (London: Whittaker, 1845).

3 This specific translation is from Gooch, *History and Historians*, p. 78. For a translation of this and two other important methodological statements, see Fritz Stern (ed.), *The Varieties of History: From Voltaire to the Present*, 2nd edn (London: Macmillan, 1970), pp. 54–62.

4 Quoted in Gooch, *History and Historians*, p. 78.

5 Handbooks of historical method produced since the nineteenth century show a remarkable continuity in their prescriptions. Compare for example C. V. Langlois and C. Seignobos, *Introduction to the Study of History*, 1st edn 1898 (London: Frank Cass, 1966). John Martin Vincent, *Historical Research: An Outline of Theory and Practice* (New York: Burt Franklin, 1974) 1st edn 1911. G. Kitson Clark, *The Critical Historian* (London: Heinemann, 1967). J. H. Hexter, *The History Primer* (New York: Basic Books, 1971). Marwick, *New Nature of History*, especially pp. 152–238.

6 The great work on historicism is Friedrich Meinecke, *Historism: The Rise of a New Historical Outlook* (New York: Herder & Herder, 1972) 1st edn 1936. See also G. G. Iggers, 'Historicism', in P. P. Weiner (ed.), *Dictionary of the History of Ideas*, 5 vols (New York: Charles Scribner's, 1973), vol. II, pp. 456–64. Arnaldo Momigliano, 'Historicism revisited', in *Essays in Ancient and Modern Historiography* (Oxford: Oxford University Press, 1977).

7 Quoted in Gooch, *History and Historians*, p. 99.

8 Ibid. p. 100.

9 Evans, *In Defence of History*, pp. 116–23.

10 Quoted in Kenyon, *History Men*, p. 155.

11 Kenyon, *The History Men*, pp. 149–208 gives a good account of this process in Britain. The outstanding survey of the process in the United States is Peter Novick, *That Noble Dream: The 'Objectivity Question' and the American Historical Profession* (Cambridge, MA: Harvard University Press, 1988).

12 G. G. Iggers, *Historiography in the Twentieth Century: From Scientific Objectivity to the Postmodern Challenge* (Hanover, NH: University Press of New England, 1997), pp. 23–30 gives a short account of his argument. For a longer one, see Iggers and Powell, *Leopold Von Ranke and the Shaping of the Historical Discipline*.

13 For Acton's historical thought and its links to his wider philosophy, see John Nurser, *The Reign of Conscience: Individual, Church and State in Lord Acton's History of Liberty* (New York: Garland, 1987), especially pp. 132–58; and J. Rufus Fears (ed), *Selected Writings of Lord Acton Volume III: Essays in the Study and Writing of History* (Indianapolis: Liberty Fund, 1985).

14 For a short survey of the 'Prussian School' in English, the best guide is still Gooch, *History and Historians*, pp. 130–55.

15 Ibid., pp. 169–85. A very good introduction to French Romantic historiography is Ceri Crossley, *French Historians and Romanticism: Thierry, Guizot, the Saint-Simonians, Quinet, Michelet* (London: Routledge, 1993). See also B. A. Haddock, *An Introduction to Historical Thought* (London: Edward Arnold, 1980), pp. 90–105.

16 Ibid., pp. 135–49. W. M. Simon, *European Positivism in the Nineteenth Century* (Ithaca, NY: Cornell University Press, 1963). Christopher Parker, *The English Historical Tradition Since 1850* (Edinburgh: John Donald, 1990), pp. 21–41, 88–93.

17 For Fustel, see Marwick, *New Nature of History*, p. 73. For programmatic statements of the positivist position from both Fustel and Bury, see Stern, *Varieties of History*, pp. 178–90, 209–26.

18 A good short introduction to Hegel for non-philosophers is P. Singer, *Hegel* (Oxford: Oxford University Press, 1983). More advanced is B. T. Wilkins, *Hegel's Philosophy of History* (Ithaca, NY: Cornell University Press, 1974).

19 For Croce, the best work is D. D. Roberts, *Benedetto Croce and the Uses of Historicism* (Berkeley, CA: University of California Press, 1987). Collingwood is enjoying something of a revival. See W. H. Dray, *History as Re-enactment: R. G. Collingwood's Idea of History* (Oxford: Oxford University Press, 1995); and M. Neilson, 'Re-enactment and reconstruction in Collingwood's philosophy of history', *History and Theory*, xx (1981), 1–31.

20 For a clear, short introduction to Dilthey and other philosophers of history, see Marnie Hughes-Warrington, *Fifty Key Thinkers on History* (London: Routledge, 2000).

▶ 3 The Transformation of Biography in Empirical History

1 Evans, *In Defence of History*, pp. 186–9.

2 Norman Gash, 'A modest defence of historical biography', in *Pillars of Government* (London: Edward Arnold, 1986), pp. 179–85. Derek Beales, 'History and

biography: An inaugural lecture', in T. C. W. Blanning and David Cannadine (eds), *History and Biography: Essays in Honour of Derek Beales* (Cambridge: Cambridge University Press, 1981), pp. 266–83.

3   Stern, *Varieties of History*, p. 101.

4   Jordanova, *History in Practice*, pp. 41–2.

5   Quoted in Hughes-Warrington, *Fifty Key Thinkers on History*, p. 103.

6   Lytton Strachey, *Eminent Victorians* (Harmondsworth: Penguin Books, 1989) 1st edn 1921. Strachey is very entertaining to read but not a true historical biographer – the 'debunking life', which he pioneered, is no more than the reverse of the 'exemplary life'.

7   On the creation of the *DNB* see the comments by the man who replaced Stephen as editor. Sidney Lee '*The Dictionary of National Biography*: A statistical account', in *Dictionary of National Biography*, vol. I, pp. v–xxii (Oxford: Oxford University Press, 1900). Dictionaries of historical biography had been a popular historical genre from the mid-eighteenth century onwards, but this was the first one done to academic standards. See also David Cannadine, 'The Dictionary of National Biography', in *The Pleasures of the Past* (Glasgow: Fontana, 1990), pp. 275–84.

8   W. Montgomery Watt, *Muhammad at Mecca* (Oxford: Oxford University Press, 1953), *Muhammad at Medina* (Oxford: Oxford University Press, 1956). M. Cook, *Muhammad* (Oxford: Oxford University Press, 1983). M. Cook and P. Crone, *Hagarism: The Making of the Islamic World* (Cambridge: Cambridge University Press, 1977). John Wansbrough, *Quranic Studies* (Oxford: Oxford University Press, 1977).

9   Pieter Geyl, *Napoleon: For and Against* (London: Yale University Press, 1949).

10 For a survey of the historiography of Lincoln, see Gabor S. Borritt and Norman O. Forness (eds), *The Historian's Lincoln: Pseudohistory, Psychohistory, and History* (Urbana: University of Illinois Press, 1988).

11 Sir Ronald Syme, *The Augustan Aristocracy* (Oxford: Clarendon Press, 1986). Sir Lewis Namier, *The Structure of Politics at the Accession of George III*, 2nd edn (London: Macmillan, 1957). Olive Banks, *Becoming a Feminist: The Social Origins of 'First Wave' Feminism* (Athens: University of Georgia Press, 1987).

12 Peter Gay, *Freud for Historians* (Oxford: Oxford University Press, 1985). David Stannard, *Shrinking History: On Freud and the Failure of Psychohistory* (Oxford: Oxford University Press, 1980). Jacques Barzun, *Clio and the Doctors: Psycho-History, Quanto-History and History* (Chicago: University of Chicago Press, 1974).

13 John Lukács, *The Hitler of History* (New York: Vintage Books, 1998). Allan Bullock, *Hitler: A Study in Tyranny* (Harmondsworth: Penguin Books, 1990), *Hitler and Stalin: Parallel Lives* (London: Fontana, 1998). Joachim C. Fest, *Hitler* (Harmondsworth: Penguin Books, 2002). Ian Kershaw, *Hitler 1889–1936: Hubris* (Harmondsworth: Penguin Books, 2001), *Hitler 1936–1945: Nemesis*

(Harmondsworth: Penguin Books, 2001), *The 'Hitler Myth'* (Oxford: Clarendon Press, 1987), *The Nazi Dictatorship* (London: Edward Arnold, 2000). The last two books show how Kershaw was led to a biographical approach despite starting with an institutional one.

14 For Kershaw's account of this, see *Hitler: Hubris*, pp. xi–xiii. It is worth contrasting Kershaw's combination of institutional and biographical approaches with the work of Michael Burleigh. See Michael Burleigh, *The Third Reich: A New History*, (Basingstoke: Macmillan – now Palgrave Macmillan, 2000).

15 John Morley, *The Life of William Ewart Gladstone, MP*, 3 vols (London: Macmillan, 1903). Sir Philip Magnus, *Gladstone: A Biography* (Harmondsworth: Penguin Books, 2001). H. C. G. Matthew, *Gladstone 1809–1898* (Oxford: Clarendon Press, 1997). Richard Shannon, *Gladstone: Peel's Inheritor 1809–1865*, 1st edn 1982 (Harmondsworth: Penguin Books, 1999), *Gladstone: Heroic Minister 1865–1898* (Harmondsworth: Penguin Books, 2000).

16 Carlo Ginzburg, *The Cheese and the Worms: The Cosmos of a Sixteenth-Century Miller* (London: 1980); Natalie Zemon-Davis, *The Return of Martin Guerre* (Cambridge, MA: Harvard University Press, 1983); Robert Finlay, 'The refashioning of Martin Guerre', *American Historical Review*, xcIII (1988), 553–71. See also Evans, *In Defence of History*, pp. 245–7; and Marwick, *New Nature of History*, pp. 138–43.

▶ 4 The Empirical History of Institutions

1 Marwick, *New Nature of History*, pp. 172–9.
2 Ibid., pp. 74–5. Butterfield, *The Whig Interpretation of History* (London: Bell, 1931) is the classic description. See also John Vincent, *An Intelligent Person's Guide to History* (London: Duckworth, 1995) pp. 57–61.
3 John Cannon et al. (eds), *The Blackwell Dictionary of Historians* (Oxford: Basil Blackwell, 1988), pp. 134–5.
4 Ibid., p. 368.
5 F. M. Powicke, 'Sir Paul Vinogradoff', *English Historical Review*, xxvi (1926), 236–43.
6 J. R. Cameron, *F. W. Maitland and the History of English Law* (Norman, OK: University of Oklahoma Press, 1961). G. R. Elton, *F. W. Maitland* (London: Weidenfield & Nicolson, 1985).
7 Pocock, *Ancient Constitution and Feudal Law*, is the main work. See also S. T. Kliger, *The Goths in England: A Study in Seventeenth- and Eighteenth-Century Thought* (Cambridge, MA: Harvard University Press, 1952). For Prynne, see William Lamont, *Marginal Prynne, 1600–1669* (London: Routledge & Kegan Paul, 1963), especially pp. 137–234.

8 Marwick, *New Nature of History*, pp. 74–5. Kenyon, *History Men*, pp. 70–87.
9 Ibid., pp. 154–64. Vincent, *Intelligent Person's Guide to History*, pp. 87–9. For a
   more critical perspective, see Parker, *English Historical Tradition*, pp. 31–45.
10 G. R. Elton, *The Tudor Revolution in Government: Administrative Changes in the
   Reign of Henry VIII* (Cambridge: Cambridge University Press, 1953). C. Coleman
   and D. Starkey (eds), *Revolution Reassessed: Revisions in the History of Tudor
   Government and Administration* (Oxford: Oxford University Press, 1986).
12 D. V. Glass and D. E. C. Eversley (eds), *Population and History* (London: Edward
   Arnold, 1965). P. Laslett and R. Wall (eds), *Household and Family in Past Time*
   (Cambridge: Cambridge University Press, 1972). E. A. Wrigley and R. S.
   Schofield, *The Population History of England 1541–1871: A Reconstruction*
   (London: Edward Arnold, 1981). Michael Anderson, *Approaches to the History
   of the Western Family 1500–1914* (London: Macmillan, 1980).
13 For the 'thesis', see Philippe Aries, *Centuries of Childhood: A Social History of
   Family Life* (New York: Random House, 1965). Edward Shorter, *The Making
   of the Modern Family* (New York: Basic Books, 1977). Lawrence Stone, *The
   Family, Sex and Marriage in England, 1500–1800* (Harmondsworth: Penguin,
   1979). For the empirical counterblast, see Linda Pollock, *Forgotten Children:
   Parent-Child Relations from 1500 to 1900* (Cambridge: Cambridge University
   Press, 1985). Stephen Ozment, *Flesh and Spirit: Private Life in Early Modern
   Germany* (New York: Penguin Books, 2001), *When Fathers Ruled: Family Life In
   Reformation Europe* (Cambridge, MA: Harvard University Press, 1985), and
   Ancestors: The Loving Family in Old Europe (Cambridge, MA: Harvard University
   Press, 2001).
14 Norval Morris and David J. Rothman (eds), *The Oxford History of the Prison*
   (Oxford; Oxford University Press, 1998), particularly the essays by McConville
   (pp. 117–50) and Spierenburg (pp. 44–70). For Foucault's position, see Michel
   Foucault, *Discipline and Punish: The Birth of the Prison*, trans. Alan Sheridan
   (New York: Vintage Books, 1979).

▶ 5 Political History – The Master Topic?

1 Thucydides, Rex Warner (trans.), *The History of the Peloponnesian War* (Harmondsworth: Penguin, 1954).
2 J. H. Hexter, 'Fernand Braudel and the Monde Braudellien', in *On Historians*
   (London: Collins, 1979), pp. 61–148.
3 C. Haigh 'The recent historiography of the English Reformation', *Historical
   Journal*, xxv (1982), 995–1007.
4 Niall Ferguson (ed.), *Virtual History: Alternatives and Counterfactuals* (Basingstoke: Macmillan – now Palgrave Macmillan, 1998).

5   Vincent, *An Intelligent Person's Guide to History*, pp. 35–44. Elton, *Return to Essentials*, pp. 92–4.

6   Ibid., p. 119.

7   D. M. Fahey 'Gardiner and Usher in Perspective', *Journal of Historical Studies*, I (1967/8), 137–50.

8   Alastair MacLachlan, *The Rise and Fall of Revolutionary England: An Essay on the Fabrication of Seventeenth-Century History* (Basingstoke: Macmillan – now Palgrave Macmillan, 1997).

9   J. C. D. Clark, *Revolution and Rebellion: State and Society in England in the Seventeenth and Eighteenth Centuries* (Cambridge: Cambridge University Press, 1986), pp. 1–23.

10   Ibid., *passim*. MacLachlan, *Rise and Fall*, pp. 210–51. J. H. Hexter, 'The historical method of Christopher Hill', in *On Historians*, pp. 227–54.

11   J. H. Hexter, 'The Early Stuarts and Parliament: Old hat and the nouvelle vague', *Parliamentary History*, I (1982), 181–215, and 'Power struggle, Parliament, and liberty in early Stuart England', *Journal of Modern History*, L (1978), 4–5.

12   J. C. D. Clark, *Revolution and Rebellion, passim. English Society 1688–1832: Ideology, Social Structure and Political Practice During the Ancien Regime* (Cambridge: Cambridge University Press, 1985). The second edition, *English Society 1660–1832* (Cambridge: Cambridge University Press, 2000) is so extensively altered as to be effectively a different book.

13   Alfred Cobban, *Aspects of the French Revolution* (London: Jonathan Cape, 1968). W. Doyle, *Origins of the French Revolution* (Oxford: Oxford University Press, 1980).

14   G. V. Taylor, 'Types of capitalism in eighteenth-century France', *English Historical Review*, LXIX (1964), 478–97. 'Non-capitalist wealth and the origins of the French Revolution', *American Historical Review*, LXXII (1967), 469–96. 'Revolutionary and nonrevolutionary content in the cahiers of 1789: An interim report', *French Historical Studies*, VII (1972), 479–502. François Furet, *Interpreting the French Revolution* (Cambridge: Cambridge University Press, 1981).

15   MacLachlan, *Rise and Fall*, p. 250.

▶ 6   Economic History and Empiricism

1   Vincent, *An Intelligent Person's Guide to History*, pp. 93–102. Stern, *Varieties of History*, pp. 304–13.

2   D. C. Coleman, *History and the Economic Past: An Account of the Rise and Decline of Economic History in Britain* (Oxford: Clarendon Press, 1987), p. 5.

3   Ibid., pp. 19–28. N. B. Harte (ed.), *The Study of Economic History* (London: Cass, 1971).

4 Quoted in ibid., p. 30.

5 David Hart, *Class Analysis, Slavery and the Industrial Theory of History in French Liberal Thought, 1814–1830: The Radical Liberalism of Charles Comte and Charles Dunoyer*, at http://arts.adelaide.edu.au/person/Dhart/classicalliberalism/ComteDunoyer/index.htm.

6 For information and resources on all of these figures, see the *History of Economic Thought Website*, at http://cepa.newschool.edu/het/index.htm.

7 Ibid.

8 Ibid. gives access to the text of Cliffe Leslie's article and other writings.

9 Coleman, *History and the Economic Past*, pp. 44–8. Sir William Ashley, *Surveys Historic and Economic* (New York: Kelley 1st edn 1900, 1966), pp. 1–37.

10 Coleman, *History and the Economic Past*, pp. 37–9, Harte, *Study of Economic History*, pp. xi–xxxix. T. C. Barker, 'The beginnings of the Economic History Society', *Economic History Review*, 2nd ser. xxx (1977), 1–19.

11 Quoted in Coleman, *History and the Economic Past*, p. 45.

12 Ibid., pp. 73–7.

13 Ibid., pp. 63–92 looks at Clapham's work and the debate between what the author terms 'Reformists and neutralists'. J. H. Clapham, 'Of empty economic boxes', *Economic Journal*, xxxii (1922), 305–14.

14 Peter Lindert, 'Unequal living standards', in Roderick Floud and Deirdre McCloskey (eds), *The Economic History of Britain Since 1700: Volume I, 1700–1860*, pp. 357–86. See also the title essay in D. C. Coleman, *Myth, History and the Industrial Revolution* (London: Hambledon Press, 1992), pp. 1–42.

15 Lindert, 'Unequal living standards'.

16 Alun Howkins, 'Agrarian histories and agricultural revolutions', in William Lamont (ed.), *Historical Controversies and Historians* (London: UCL Press, 1998), pp. 81–92.

17 Nick Crafts, 'The industrial revolution', in Floud and McCloskey, *Economic History*, Vol. I, pp. 44–59. P. Deane and W. A. Cole, *British Economic Growth, 1688–1959*, 2nd edn (Cambridge: Cambridge University Press, 1967).

18 R. M. Hartwell, 'Was there an industrial revolution?', *Social Science History*, xiv (1990), 567–76. M. Berg and P. Hudson, 'Rehabilitating the Industrial Revolution', *Economic History Review*, xlv (1992), 24–50.

19 For a defence of Tawney, see William Lamont, 'R. H. Tawney: "Who did not write a single work which can be trusted"?', in Lamont, *Historical Controversies*, pp. 109–20.

20 Gad Heuman, 'Slavery, the slave trade and abolition', in Robin W. Winks (ed.), *The Oxford History of the British Empire Volume V: Historiography*, pp. 315–26.

21 R. W. Fogel, 'The "New economic history": Its findings and methods', *Economic History Review*, 2nd ser. xix (1966), 642–57. J. R. T. Hughes, 'Fact and theory in economic history', *Explorations in Entrepreneurial History*, iii (1966),

75–100. P. Temin, 'The future of "new economic history"', *Journal of Interdisciplinary History*, XII (1981–2), 179–97. J. Topolski, 'The model method in economic history', *Journal of European Economic History*, I (1972), 713–26.

22 D. C. North, 'Structure and performance: The task of economic history', *Journal of Economic Literature*, XVI (1978) 963–78. D. C. North and R. P. Thomas, *The Rise of the Western World*, (Cambridge: Cambridge University Press, 1973). E. L. Jones, *The European Miracle: Environments, Economics and Geopolitics in the History of Europe and Asia* (Cambridge: Cambridge University Press, 1987). David S. Landes, *The Wealth and Poverty of Nations: Why Some Are So Rich and Some So Poor* (London: Little Brown, 1998).

23 I. Wallerstein, *The Modern World System, Vol. I: Capitalist Agriculture and the Origins of the European World Economy in the 16th Century* (New York: 1974); *Vol. II: Mercantilism and the Consolidation of the European World Economy, 1600–1750* (New York: 1980). T. Skocpol, 'Wallerstein's world capitalist system', *American Journal of Sociology*, LXXXII (1977), 1075–90. Fernand Braudel, *Material Civilisation and Capitalism*, trans. Sian Reynolds, *Vol. I: The Structures of Everyday Life; Vol. II: The Wheels of Commerce; Vol. III: The Perspective of the World* (London: Fontana, 1985). Janet Abu-Lughod, *Before European Hegemony: The World System, 1250–1350* (Oxford: Oxford University Press, 1989).

▶ **7 History of Ideas – The Empirical Turn?**

1 Felix Gilbert, *History: Politics or Culture? Reflections on Ranke and Burckhardt.* (Princeton: Princeton University Press, 1990).

2 Harry Elmer Barnes, *A History of Historical Writing*, 2nd edn (New York: Dover Publications, 1963), pp. 310–29.

3 A. O. Lovejoy, *The Great Chain of Being* (Cambridge, MA: Harvard University Press, 1936), *Essays in the History of Ideas* (New York: George Brazillier, 1955), particularly pp. 1–13, 'The historiography of ideas'.

4 The best guide to the kind of work that Lovejoy's ideas led to is Philip P. Wiener (ed.), *Dictionary of the History of Ideas: Studies of Selected Pivotal Ideas*, 5 vols (New York: Charles Scribner's, 1973).

5 Marwick, *New Nature of History*, p. 142. MacLachlan, *Rise and Fall*, pp. 284–9.

6 John Dunn, *The Political Thought of John Locke* (Cambridge: Cambridge University Press, 1969). Richard Ashcraft, *Locke's Two Treatises of Government* (London: Unwin Hyman, 1987). R. Ashcraft and M. Goldsmith, 'Locke, revolution principles and the formation of Whig ideology', *Historical Journal*, XXVI (1983), 773–800.

7 James Tully (ed.), *Meaning and Context: Quentin Skinner and his Critics* (Cambridge: Polity Press, 1988). M. Richter, 'Reconstituting the history of

political languages: Pocock, Skinner, and the Geschichliche Grundbegriffe', *History and Theory*, xxix (1990), 38–70.

8 Tully, *Meaning and Context*, pp. 7–25.

9 Ibid., pp. 29–78.

10 J. H. Hexter, ' Republic, virtue, liberty and the political universe of J. G. A. Pocock', in *On Historians*, pp. 255–304.

11 J. G. A. Pocock, *Virtue, Commerce, and History* (Cambridge: Cambridge University Press, 1985). Isaac Kramnick, *Republicanism and Bourgeois Radicalism: Political Ideology in Late Eighteenth-Century England and America* (Ithaca, NY: Cornell University Press, 1990).

12 Tully, *Meaning and Context*, pp. 156–93.

13 David Wooton (ed.), *Divine Right and Democracy: An Anthology of Political Writing in Stuart England* (Harmondsworth: Penguin, 1986), pp. 11–12.

14 Elton, *Return to Essentials*, pp. 37–9.

15 Melvin Richter, *The History of Political and Social Concepts: A Critical Introduction* (Oxford: Oxford University Press, 1997). Reinhart Koselleck, *Critique and Crises: Enlightenment and the Pathogenesis of Modern Society* (Cambridge, MA: MIT Press, 1988).

16 L. Fèbvre, *The Problem of Unbelief in the Sixteenth Century: The Religion of Rabelais,* (Cambridge, MA: 1983). P. H. Hutton, ' The history of mentalitees: The new map of cultural history', *History and Theory*, xx (1981), 237–59.

▶ Conclusions

1 Beverley Southgate, *Why Bother With History?: Ancient, Modern, and Postmodern Motivations* (Harlow: Pearson, 2000).

2 Alun Munslow, *The Routledge Companion to Historical Studies* (London: Routledge, 2000). C. Behan McCullagh, *The Truth of History* (London: Routledge, 1998). Paul Ricoer, *History and Truth: Essays*, trans. Charles A. Kebbley (Evanston, IL: Northwestern University Press, 1966).

3 See, for example, Richard Evans, *In Defence of History*, pp. 219–23, 249–53.

Further Reading

▶ Introduction

Arnold, John H., *History: A Very Short Introduction* (Oxford: Oxford University Press, 2000): exactly what the title says, very well done with examples.

Carr, Edward Hallet, *What is History?*, 3rd edn (Basingstoke: Palgrave – now Palgrave Macmillan, 2001): still well worth reading as the exposition of a moderate position, influenced by theory (Marxism) and relativist but still ultimately empirical. This edition contains material Carr was going to use in the projected revision of his 1961 work.

Diamond, Jared, *Guns, Germs, and Steel* (New York: Vintage, 1998): contains an excellent discussion of the relation between history as an enterprise and 'soft' sciences. The work itself is an outstanding example of history as science in the wider sense of the term.

Elton, Geoffrey Rudolph, *The Practice of History*, 2nd edn (Oxford: Blackwells, 2001): the more robust empiricist line. This edition has a valuable commentary by Richard Evans.

Evans, Richard J., *In Defence of History*, 2nd edn (London: Granta, 2001): a sharp attack on the more extreme postmodernist position and defence of history as a truth-seeking exercise.

Hobsbawm, Eric, *On History* (London: Weidenfeld & Nicolson, 1997): a collection of essays, several of which defend the empirical approach from a Marxist position.

Jenkins, Keith, *Re-Thinking History* (London: Routledge, 1991): a short introduction to the postmodernist position.

Jordanova, Ludmilla, *History in Practice* (London: Edward Arnold, 2000): clearly written book that steers a middle course between the postmodernists and their more aggressive critics.

Marwick, Arthur, *The New Meaning of History: Knowledge, Evidence, Language* (Basingstoke: Palgrave – now Palgrave Macmillan, 2001): a completely recast edition of his handbook. Has discussion of the historical development of the discipline and a strongly empiricist argument against both the postmodernists and people such as Carr. Very good on the question of how far, and in what way, history is a 'science'.

Munslow, Alun, *Deconstructing History* (London: Routledge, 1997): a very good account of the three main positions on historical methodology now articulated by historians, which he terms 'reconstructionist' (Elton), 'constructionist' (Carr) and 'deconstructionist' (White). He himself espouses the last of these.

Southgate, Beverley, *History: What and Why: Ancient, Modern and Postmodern Perspectives* (London: Routledge, 1996), and *Why Bother With History? Ancient, Modern, and Postmodern Motivations* (Harlow: Pearson, 2000): moderate postmodernism and the case for history as advocacy.

White, Hayden, *The Content of the Form: Narrative Discourse and Historical Representation* (Baltimore: Johns Hopkins University Press, 1987): one of several works that launched postmodernist historical argument.

Warren, John, *The Past and Its Presenters: An Introduction to Issues in Historiography* (London: Hodder & Stoughton, 1998): like Jordanova, takes a *via media* in the debate.

Windschuttle, Keith, *The Killing of History: How Literary Critics and Social Theorists are Murdering Our Past* (New York: Free Press, 1996): the subtitle says it all really.

▶ Chapter 1

Avis, Paul, *Foundations of Modern Historical Thought: From Machiavelli to Vico* (London: Croom Helm, 1986): a series of essays on important figures, including Machiavelli, Bacon, Montaigne and Bodin. Good bibliography.

Franklin, Julian H., *Jean Bodin and the Sixteenth-Century Revolution in the Methodology of Law and History* (New York: Columbia University Press, 1961): short but packs a lot in and gives a very good entry to the otherwise complex intellectual world of sixteenth-century France.

Fussner, F. S., *The Historical Revolution: English Historical Writing and Thought, 1580–1640* (London: Routledge & Kegan Paul, 1962): covers the main figures and aspects of early modern antiquarianism. See Preston, however.

Hay, Denys, *Annalists and Historians: Western Historiography From the Eighth to the Eighteenth Centuries* (London: Methuen, 1977): covers a wide range of time, particularly good on the seventeenth and eighteenth centuries.

Kelley, Donald R., *Versions of History from Antiquity to the Enlightenment* (London: Yale University Press, 1991): a good historiographical survey. And *Foundations of Modern Historical Scholarship: Language, Law and History in the French Renaissance* (New York: Columbia University Press, 1970): the best comprehensive work on the rise of critical thought in sixteenth-century French law.

Levine, Joseph M., *Humanism and History: Origins of Modern English Historiography* (Ithaca, NY: Cornell University Press, 1987): a collection of essays that looks at the growth of the historical sense and the nature of antiquarianism.

Nadel, G. H., 'Philosophy of history before historism', *History and Theory*, III (1964), 291–315. Looks at historical thought in the eighteenth century.

Phillips, Mark Salber, *Society and Sentiment: Genres of Historical Writing in Britain, 1740–1820* (Princeton, NJ: Princeton University Press, 2000): an excellent survey of the whole range of works published under the rubric of 'history' during the late eighteenth/early nineteenth centuries.

Preston, Joseph H., 'Was there an historical revolution?', *Journal of the History of Ideas*, XXXVIII (1977), 353–64. Read along with Fussner.

▶ Chapter 2

Bentley, Michael, *Modern Historiography* (London: Routledge, 1998): a survey (taken in part from a much larger work) of the range and development of history in modern times.

Butterfield, Herbert, *Man on His Past* (Cambridge: Cambridge University Press, 1955): an old account but useful, contains examples.

Gooch, George Peabody, *History and Historians in the Nineteenth Century* (London: Longmans, Green & Co., 1913): an old work but still the best general survey of nineteenth-century historiography. Also useful because it gives an insight into how a historian of Gooch's generation viewed the development of the discipline at that time.

Hexter, J. H., *The History Primer* (New York: Basic Books, 1971). Marwick, *New Nature of History*, especially pp. 152–238.

Hughes-Warrington, Marnie, *Fifty Key Thinkers on History* (London: Routledge, 2000): very well done short biographies of important figures with suggestions for further reading. The selection is slightly idiosyncratic but very useful.

Iggers, G. G., *Historiography in the Twentieth Century: From Scientific Objectivity to the Postmodern Challenge* (London: Wesleyan University Press, 1997): starts with a good analysis of the state of historical thought at the start of the century and then traces movements up to today.

Iggers, G. G. and Von Moltke, K. (eds), *The Theory and Practice of History* (Indianapolis: Bobbs Merrill, 1973): an introduction to Ranke in his own words.

Iggers, G. G. and Powell, James, M. (eds), *Leopold Von Ranke and the Shaping of the Historical Discipline* (Syracuse, NY; 1990): a collection of essays about Ranke and his work.

Kenyon, John, *The History Men: The Historical Profession in England Since the Renaissance*, 2nd edn (London: Weidenfeld & Nicolson, 1993): clear account of the growth of professional history, with sharply drawn pen-portraits of individuals. Compare with Parker.

Meinecke, Friedrich, *Historism: The Rise of a New Historical Outlook*, 1st edn 1936 (New York: Herder and Herder, 1972): an account of the rise of historicism by a leading German historian.

Novick, Peter, *That Noble Dream: The 'Objectivity Question' and the American Historical Profession* (Cambridge: Cambridge University Press, 1988): an outstanding work that looks at the rise of organized professional history in America and its domination by Rankean ideals, and the way these came under attack.

Parker, Christopher, *The English Historical Tradition Since 1850* (Edinburgh: John Donald, 1990): covers much the same ground as Kenyon, but from a very different perspective as Parker is highly critical of the domination of the profession by empiricism and positivism.

Vincent, John, *An Intelligent Person's Guide to History* (London: Duckworth, 1995): short survey of both the nature of history and the development of the discipline. One of the best ways of seeing what is entailed by the empirical mode of history and also how persistent is has been is to look at the various handbooks that historians have produced over the years. See, in chronological order: Langlois, C. V. and Seignobos, C., *Introduction to the Study of History*, 1st edn 1898 (London: Frank Cass, 1966). Vincent, John Martin, *Historical Research: An Outline of Theory and Practice*, 1st edn 1911 (New York: Burt Franklin, 1974). Clark, G. Kitson, *The Critical Historian* (London: Heinemann, 1967).

▶ Chapter 3

For an introduction, setting out what can be gained from historical biography and how it should be done, see:

Beales, Derek, 'History and biography: An inaugural lecture', in Blanning, T. C. W. and Cannadine, David (eds), *History and Biography: Essays in Honour of Derek Beales* (Cambridge: Cambridge University Press, 1981), pp. 266–83.

Gash, Norman, 'A modest defence of historical biography', in *Pillars of Government* (London: Edward Arnold, 1986) pp. 179–85.

The best way of appreciating the impact made by empirical methods on biography is to look at examples. Three good cases are Lincoln, Hitler and Gladstone. For Lincoln, see: Borritt, Gabor S. and Forness, Norman O. (eds) *The Historian's Lincoln: Pseudohistory, Psychohistory, and History* (Urbana, IL: University of Illinois Press, 1988) which looks at the range of biographies that have appeared. The best ones to compare are, first, Sandburg, Carl, *Abraham Lincoln: The Prairie Years and The War Years* (New York: Harcourt Brace,

1984) (one volume edn – the original six volumes might be a bit much!) which is a classic 'exemplary' life. For the more recent versions, see: Randall, James G. *Lincoln the President*, 4 vols (New York: Dodd, Mead, 1945–55); Oates, Stephen B., *With Malice Towards None: The Life of Abraham Lincoln* (New York, Harper Row, 1977); and Donald, David, *Lincoln*, (New York: Simon & Schuster, 1995). In Hitler's case the survey is provided by Lukács, John, *The Hitler of History* (New York: Vintage Books, 1998), which again surveys the whole range of biographies. For historical works, see: Bullock, Allan, *Hitler: A Study in Tyranny* (Harmondsworth: Penguin Books, 1990), and *Hitler and Stalin: Parallel Lives* (London: Fontana, 1998). Fest, Joachim C. *Hitler* (Harmondsworth: Penguin Books, 2002). Kershaw, Ian, *Hitler, 1889–1936: Hubris* (Harmondsworth: Penguin Books, 2001), and *Hitler, 1936–1945: Nemesis* (Harmondsworth: Penguin Books, 2001). There is no real survey of the various biographies of Gladstone. The starting point is Morley, John, *The Life of William Ewart Gladstone, MP*, 3 vols (London: Macmillan, 1903) which is the classic work. A representative later one is Magnus, Sir Philip, *Gladstone: A Biography* (Harmondsworth: Penguin Books, 2001). For the most recent works, see: Matthew, H. C. G., *Gladstone 1809–1898* (Oxford: Clarendon Press, 1997). Shannon, Richard, *Gladstone: Peel's Inheritor 1809–1865*, 1st edn 1982 (Harmondsworth: Penguin Books, 1999), *Gladstone: Heroic Minister, 1865–1898* (Harmondsworth: Penguin Books, 2000). See also Biagini, Eugenio F., *Gladstone* (Basingstoke: Palgrave – now Palgrave Macmillan, 2000). For the debate on psychohistory, see Gay, Peter *Freud for Historians* (Oxford: Oxford University Press, 1985) which sets out the case for using psychoanalysis and Stannard, David, *Shrinking History: On Freud and the Failure of Psychohistory* (Oxford: Oxford University Press, 1980) a sharp attack on that position.

▶ Chapter 4

Again the best way of exploring this topic is to actually see how historiographical debates work and how ideas about institutions develop with research. The nineteenth-century debate over the history of the institutions of the British constitution is examined both in Kenyon, *History Men*, and Parker, *English Historical Tradition*. A study of the historiographical traditions is Burrow, J. W., *A Liberal Descent: Victorian Historians and the English Past* (Cambridge: Cambridge University Press, 1981). A good entry into the work of one of the great institutional historians is Schuyler, R. L. (ed.), *Frederick William Maitland, Historian: Selections From His Writings* (Berkeley, CA: University of California Press 1987). Elton, G. R., *Frederick William Maitland: A Life* (London: Weidenfeld & Nicolson, 1985) has examples of his work and methods. Cameron,

James R., *Frederick William Maitland and the History of English Law* (London: Greenwood Press, 1977) surveys the development of this form of institutional history and Maitland's part in it. It is worth looking at his great work to gain some notion of the method employed. Pollock, Sir F. and Maitland, F. W., *The History of English Law Before the Time of Edward I* (Cambridge: Cambridge University Press, 1968). An example of institutional history that clearly shows how the inductive cycle works is the debate over the 'Tudor revolution' thesis of G. R. Elton. The initial thesis is in Elton, G. R., *The Tudor Revolution in Government: Administrative Changes in the Reign of Henry VIII* (Cambridge: Cambridge University Press, 1953). The initial reaction can be found in Williams, P. and Harriss, G. L., 'A revolution in Tudor history?', *Past and Present*, xxv (1963), 3–58; with a summing up of later criticisms in Coleman, C. and Starkey, D. (eds), *Revolution Reassessed: Revisions in the History of Tudor Government and Administration* (Oxford: Oxford University Press, 1986). The debate over family organization and relations clearly demonstrates the difference between empirical and non-empirical approaches. First look at Aries, Philippe, *Centuries of Childhood: A Social History of Family Life* (New York: Random House, 1965); and Shorter, Edward, *The Making of the Modern Family* (New York: Basic Books, 1977); and Stone, Lawrence, *The Family, Sex and Marriage in England 1500–1800* (Harmondsworth: Penguin, 1979). Try to see what sources they use and (more significantly) what they do not use. You should also try to determine where some of their starting assumptions come from. The response is in Pollock, Linda, *Forgotten Children: Parent-Child Relations from 1500 to 1900* (Cambridge: Cambridge University Press, 1985); and Ozment, Stephen, *Flesh and Spirit: Private Life in Early Modern Germany* (New York: Penguin Books, 2001), *When Fathers Ruled: Family Life In Reformation Europe* (Cambridge, MA: Harvard University Press, 1985), and *Ancestors: The Loving Family in Old Europe* (Cambridge MA: Harvard University Press, 2001). Look at the sources used, how they are used, and compare them with the earlier work of Stone, Aries and Shorter.

▶ Chapter 5

Clark, J. C. D., *English Society, 1688–1832: Ideology, Social Structure and Political Practice During the Ancien Regime* (Cambridge: Cambridge University Press, 1985).

Clark, J. C. D., *Revolution and Rebellion: State and Society in England in the Seventeenth and Eighteenth Centuries* (Cambridge: Cambridge University Press, 1986): an account of the revisionist view of the seventeenth and eighteenth centuries by a participant. Highly polemical. See Pocock below for a different view.

Clark, J. C. D., *English Society, 1660–1832*, (Cambridge: Cambridge University Press, 2000): there are so many changes from the first to second editions of this book that it should count as two separate works. The first edition is a compendium of the findings of the revisionists. The second is more restrained and shows how those findings had become incorporated into a new narrative, which the earlier work had done much to create. For an indication of how far a new 'standard account' had appeared, see one outstanding textbook, O'Gorman, Frank, *The Long Eighteenth Century: British Political and Social History, 1688– 1832* (London: Edward Arnold, 1997).

Elton, G. R., *Political History: Principles and Practice* (London: Allen Lane, 1970): a characteristically robust articulation of the traditional position.

Elton, G. R., *Return to Essentials: Some Reflections on the Present State of Historical Study* (Cambridge: Cambridge University Press, 1991): as well as an intemperate attack on postmodernism, this contains a vigorous defence of the importance of political history for the historical enterprise in general.

Fahey, D. M., 'Gardiner and Usher in Perspective', *Journal of Historical Studies*, I (1967–8), 137–50. An account of the methods of Gardiner and the attack made on them in 1915 by the American historian R. G. Usher.

Ferguson, Niall (ed.), *Virtual History: Alternatives and Counterfactuals* (Basingstoke: Macmillan – now Palgrave Macmillan, 1998): explores the role of counterfactual thinking in political history. The introduction is a sustained attack on determinist theories of politics.

Fulbrook, Mary, 'The English Revolution and the revisionist revolt', *Social History*, VII (1982), 249–64. Surveys the situation at the height of the revisionist response to the earlier model-driven approach.

Furet, François, *Interpreting the French Revolution* (Cambridge: Cambridge University Press, 1981): a summary of the results of the previous 20 years of research on the events of the Revolution.

MacLachlan, Alastair, *The Rise and Fall of Revolutionary England: An Essay on the Fabrication of Seventeenth-Century History* (London: Macmillan, 1966): an outstanding historiographical survey that traces the rise of a model of 'revolution' and its application to the history of seventeenth-century England and its undermining by empirical research. Also points out the problems with the fragmented picture that resulted.

Pocock, J. G. A., '1660 and all that: Whig hunting, ideology and historiography in the work of Jonathan Clark', *Cambridge Review*, CVIII (October 1987), 125–8. A response to Clark's earlier surveys.

Richardson, R. C., *The Debate on the English Revolution*, 3rd edn (Manchester: Manchester University Press, 1998): a survey of the historiography of this event and the movements in interpretation. Good for seeing how the destructive phase of research has led more recently to a more chastened narrative that incorporates the findings of the empirical researchers without abandoning all of the earlier account.

▶ Chapter 6

History of Economic Thought Website at:

http://cepa.newschool.edu/het/index.htm: this is an outstanding site with material on many economic historians as well as pure economists.

Clapham, J. H. *An Economic History of Modern Britain: Vol. I: The Early Railway Age, 1820–1850* (Cambridge: Cambridge University Press, 1926), *Vol. II: Free Trade and Steel, 1850–1886* (Cambridge: Cambridge University Press, 1932), *Vol. III: Machines and National Rivalries, 1887–1914. With an Epilogue, 1914–1929* (Cambridge: Cambridge University Press, 1938).

Coleman, D. C., *History and the Economic Past: An Account of the Rise and Decline of Economic History in Britain* (Oxford: Clarendon Press, 1987): a clear account of the origins of economic history and its development as an academic subject in Britain.

Coleman, D. C., *Myth, History, and the Industrial Revolution* (London: Hambledon Press, 1992): the title essay is an excellent introduction to the way the idea of an 'industrial revolution' came about and how it shaped research that then undermined the myths that were associated with it.

Floud, Roderick and McCloskey, Deirdre (eds), *The Economic History Of Britain Since 1700*, 2nd edn, Vol. I 1700–1860; Vol. II 1860–1939; Vol. III 1939–92 (Cambridge: Cambridge University Press, 1994).

Comparison of the two works reveals the nature of research in economic history and the way it has led to a growth of knowledge.

Lamont, William (ed.), *Historical Controversies and Historians* (London: UCL Press, 1998): contains two relevant essays, one on agricultural economic historiography, the other on Tawney.

For a survey of the move to the 'new economic history' and the (alleged) rise of a more theoretical approach, see:

Fogel, R. W., 'The "New economic history": its findings and methods', *Economic History Review*, 2nd ser. XIX (1966), 642–57. Hughes, J. R. T. 'Fact and theory in economic history', *Explorations in Entrepreneurial History*, III (1966), 75–100. Temin, P. 'The future of "new economic history" ', *Journal of Interdisciplinary History*, XII (1981–2), 179–97. Topolski, J., 'The model method in economic history', *Journal of European Economic History,* I (1972), 713–26. See also the respectful exchange in Elton, G. R. and Fogel, R. W., *Which Road to The Past? Two Views of History* (London: Yale University Press, 1983).

▶ **Chapter 7**

Gilbert, Felix, *History: Politics or Culture? Reflections on Ranke and Burckhardt* (Princeton, NJ: Princeton University Press, 1990): looks at the origins of cultural history and the supposed divisions between it and the Rankean approach.

Hutton, P. H., ' The history of mentalitees: The new map of cultural history', *History and Theory*, xx (1981), 237–59: introduction to this area of Annales type history.

Lovejoy, A. O., *The Great Chain of Being* (Cambridge, MA: Harvard University Press, 1936.): essential reading because of its influence on the historiography and worth reading in its own right.

Melvin Richter, *The History of Political and Social Concepts: A Critical Introduction* (Oxford: Oxford University Press, 1997): an introduction to another approach to history of ideas.

Richter, Melvin, 'Reconstituting the history of political languages: Pocock, Skinner, and the Geschichliche Grundbegriffe', *History and Theory*, xxix (1990), 38–70: another response to the Cambridge school.

Tully, James (ed.), *Meaning and Context: Quentin Skinner and his Critics* (Cambridge: Polity Press, 1988): collects all of Skinner's methodological articles and several criticisms of them, together with a specially written response from Skinner.

Wiener, Philip P. (ed.), *Dictionary of the History of Ideas: Studies of Selected Pivotal Ideas*, 5 vols (New York: Charles Scribner's, 1973): a massive work made up of many excellent essays that provide a good introduction to mainstream history of ideas.

Index